THE
Playful Leader's
TOOLKIT

Creating a legacy of joy and magic...
in ruby slippers

BY RACHEL SUPALLA M.ED

Edited by Lil Barcaski

Published by: GWN Publishing
www.GWNPublishing.com

Cover Design: Kristina Conatser

ISBN: 978-1-965971-08-6

DEDICATION

To Eric, my rock, my safe place, and my partner in all of life's adventures. Your unwavering support, patience, and love fuel me every day.

To my incredible children—Abbie, Allie, Zack, and Trent—each of you has shaped my journey in ways I could never have imagined. Abbie, your passion and dedication to DKZ and the children we serve is truly magical; watching you lead with your heart fills me with pride. Allie, I love watching you step into motherhood—it is beautiful to see you love and nurture so deeply. Zack, your sweet, empathetic soul reminds me of the power of kindness and resilience. Trent, your joyful spirit and constant reminder to be a friend to all inspire me every day. And to Baby Zeke, my hope for the future—you are a shining light, and I can't wait to see the adventures life holds for you.

TABLE OF CONTENTS

STEPPING ONTO THE YELLOW BRICK ROAD

"I think I'll buy a magazine," I said to my good friend Melissa.

"Yeah, great. I'll grab us some waters," she replied and left me examining the various covers that were staring back at me from their place on the rack. There were dozens of choices on subjects from crafts to sports, home décor to auto repair, country living to coastal cottages, and fashion to finance. *C'mon, Rachel...pick one. It's not that hard!*

But I couldn't. Instead, I just stood there, frozen in place and simply could not choose a magazine. *What is happening? Am I losing it?* My heart started to race and my cheeks flushed, hot tears welling up in my eyes.

In that moment, I discovered that I had become a person I didn't recognize. I didn't know what kind of magazine I wanted because I wasn't clear about anything I wanted. All I had been doing was working on my business nearly non-stop and barely staying afloat at home. I couldn't make a simple, menial choice. Overwhelm consumed me and that moment was my first real understanding of its weight.

I was at an extreme crossroads in my life. I had been a stay-at-home supermom and a homeschooling mom. From there, I became a preschool teacher mom and then a business owner. Suddenly, add to that, I was now a career woman and entrepreneur and things were moving at lightning speed. For most of our married life, my husband was the sole breadwinner, and I was his number one cheerleader. Don't get me wrong; I loved the journey my life had taken. It had been fast and exciting, however, somewhere amidst all the chaos and noise, I lost myself. I had bigger decisions to make than what magazine to pull off a shelf.

My husband and I met when we were freshmen in high school, and we were high school sweethearts. We were the stereotypical, cliché, football player and cheerleader couple. I idolized him in every way and all I wanted was to grow up, become his wife and the mother of his children. I did exactly that, my dreams came true, but I found myself wondering what was next? Everything was changing and I felt an incredible stirring in my soul that I didn't know what to do with. I began to pay attention to it and that unsettling anxiety.

Standing there, paralyzed, zoning out, a 33-year-old woman with four children under the age of 10 and a growing business, it hit me that it was time to decide which path to take next. Do I stay where I am and hold onto the years spent mostly changing diapers, running the PTA, sewing Halloween costumes, and being Mary Poppins at home? Or do I launch headlong into this fairly new, unknown, and scary path that could lead to a bright future for me and my family? I felt like Julia Roberts in *Runaway Bride*, needing to discover how she liked her eggs cooked and everything that went along with that decision.

So, I decided to take the road less traveled (at least less traveled in my life to that point), which, for the sake of this book, we will call the *Yellow Brick Road*, symbolizing my leadership and entrepreneurial journey. Remember that Dorothy took the first step on to that iconic path with pure blind faith that it would lead her to the much touted Emerald City and the Wizard who would get her home. I think all entrepreneurs take those first steps with the same hopeful dreams. We all want to reach a goal of some sort, one that feels like home, one that fulfills the purpose we see for ourselves, and hopefully, helps other people into the bargain.

In this book, I will share with you the things I learned, mistakes and wins alike, and hopefully, it will help you as you move along your own path with more clarity and ease.

Some of you may relate to things about my story that will ring true for you. For one thing, I am and always will be a mom. I didn't put away my Mary Poppins umbrella completely, knowing that I will always be a mommy first, but I had to reinvent myself in other ways. For a while, I felt I had to fake it until I made it. And boy, there were times when I surely did fake it. There was a bit of a grieving process at first, too. Sometimes I wasn't able to be quite the supermom I'd always prided myself on being. And I was wearing more hats than ever before, which was exhausting. I felt the guilt that lots of moms tell me they feel when they step into big careers, wondering if I was enough in any capacity, doing enough for both my family and my budding businesses. But that was 11 years ago, and I can see myself more clearly and accept my successes, acknowledge my failures, and take life as it is in stride. I've created a balance that I'm proud of and a life I love. Now, as a

44-year-old woman who has learned a lot along the *Yellow Brick Road*, I am excited to share my journey with you.

I wrote this book for all the moms, women, current and aspiring leaders, and entrepreneurs out there to let you know that change is okay. When you feel stuck and need to reinvent yourself or are ready to take a chance, it's always better to do so than to not try at all. This book is for those of you who are ready to embrace the unknown and forge a new path toward greatness, to pick a magazine and choose a direction. Let's take this journey together.

My friend returned to find me still staring at the magazines.

"You okay?" she asked.

"No, but I will be," I answered and I meant it.

CHAPTER 1

THE CASE FOR PLAY IN LEADERSHIP

"The Single Secret to a Leader's Success is Play."

During the height of the pandemic, our childcare center was a whirlwind of challenges and uncertainty. Every day, I arrived before the children, my schedule packed from morning till night. Despite my tireless efforts, something felt deeply off. Our preschool was attended mostly on Zoom. The staff meetings had to be on Zoom as well because we are a multi-site organization and we could not cross-contaminate the facilities, so the staff from each school met weekly online. The camaraderie we normally felt, the energy of being in one room, was lacking.

Just prior to the pandemic, we had grown from the basement of my home, to three locations and all of them were full and thriving. We were in the middle of building a brand new school and planned to double the capacity of our flagship location. It was exciting, and our efforts had been in progress for a while. When the pandemic hit, we were about six weeks away from our building completion and the opening of our new school.

Then overnight, we had to readjust the way we did nearly everything. We still had one-third enrollment of our students attending school in person, and the majority of the parents still wanted to have their children continue to be educated, so they continued to pay full price. For the preschoolers, we sent home kits and came up with fun activities—not just having them sit in front of the computer to listen to a story. We offered a hybrid model of in-person and Zoom for all the other grades. All of this led us to being more task-oriented and less open and fun. We were all missing the energy of classrooms full of kids, and it put a damper on our teachers with the lack of interactivity. We did what we could to keep our playful model, but it wasn't easy. My goal was to keep everyone employed, and we managed to do so. Now, I needed to keep us all engaged.

One Wednesday morning, I walked into the team room for our weekly meeting. The room, usually filled with laughter and lively conversation, was eerily quiet, and the atmosphere felt cold. My team, typically beaming with enthusiasm, looked worn out and disengaged. My heart sank as I realized the spark that once defined our center was fading.

As I went through the meeting agenda, the troubling signs were impossible to ignore. Creativity in lesson planning was dwindling, the teachers' patience was thinning, and the children seemed less engaged. The center's joyful, magical atmosphere was slipping away, replaced by a sense of routine drudgery. "It's only a season," I told my team and myself, but deep down, I was at a loss.

We had a talented team and ample resources, but the relentless pace and pressure of the pandemic had taken a toll. The center's environment had become all work and no play, for both the children and the staff. I felt the creeping shadows of burnout, my once-bright passion for my work dimming under the constant stress and uncertainty.

One quiet afternoon, as I sat alone in my office, I reflected on my childhood. I remembered the freedom and joy of play, the spontaneous moments of creativity that had always left me feeling refreshed and inspired. Instantly, I craved the peace that play provided. I wondered when I had forgotten the importance of those moments. Suddenly, it hit me: play was not just essential for the children; it was crucial for my team and myself as well.

Determined to bring back the joy, I decided to make a change. I started small, introducing playful activities during our virtual staff meetings. We began with simple games and team-building exercises, fostering a sense of camaraderie and fun, despite the distance. Slowly but surely, I noticed a shift. The educators started to smile more, their creativity blossomed, and the atmosphere in the center began to transform, even through the screens.

I didn't stop there. I carved out time in my schedule for playful activities, both for myself and my team. We held themed dress-up days on Zoom, organized impromptu virtual dance parties with the children, and even set up relaxation kits filled with puzzles and art supplies for staff to use at home. The once rigid schedule began to include moments of spontaneous fun and laughter, helping us reconnect and recharge.

The results were astounding. The children thrived in the new, playful environment, their energy and enthusiasm infectious even through virtual interactions. The educators, too, were rejuvenated, their passion for their work rekindled. I felt the weight of burnout lift, replaced by a renewed sense of purpose and joy.

Through this journey, I discovered play was the secret to our success. It fostered creativity and innovation, enabling us to come up with fresh ideas and solutions to navigate the unprecedented challenges of the pandemic. It boosted engagement and morale, creating a positive work environment where everyone felt valued and motivated. Most importantly, play served as an antidote to burnout, providing much-needed relief from stress and helping us maintain a healthy work-life balance.

Our center stood out in the community, not just for its exceptional care but for its vibrant, joyful atmosphere. Parents noticed the difference, and word spread quickly. The center became a sought-after place for both children and educators, all thanks to my realization that play was not a luxury but a necessity, especially in such trying times.

Play as a Competitive Advantage

- CREATIVITY AND INNOVATION: Play fosters creativity, allowing leaders to think outside the box and come up with innovative solutions. It breaks the monotony of routine, stimulating the brain to see problems from new perspectives.

- ENGAGEMENT AND MORALE: Incorporating play into the workplace increases employee engagement and morale. When leaders demonstrate a playful attitude, it creates a positive work environment where employees feel valued and motivated.

- TEAM BUILDING: Playful activities promote team cohesion and collaboration. Leaders who prioritize play create opportunities for team bonding, which enhances communication and trust among team members.

Play as an Antidote for Burnout

- STRESS RELIEF: Play is a natural stress reliever. Engaging in playful activities helps leaders unwind and recharge, preventing burnout by providing a necessary break from the pressures of leadership.

- WORK-LIFE BALANCE: Leaders who value play understand the importance of work-life balance. By integrating play into their lives, they set an example for their teams, promoting a culture where personal well-being is prioritized.

How Play Helps Leaders Stand Out

1. Enhanced Problem-Solving Skills:

   Play encourages divergent thinking, which is critical for effective problem-solving. Leaders who engage in play are better equipped to approach challenges with a fresh perspective, finding innovative solutions that others might miss.

2. Emotional Intelligence:

   Playful leaders often exhibit higher levels of emotional intelligence. They are more attuned to their own emotions and those of their team members, enabling them to lead with empathy and build stronger, more supportive relationships.

3. **Resilience and Adaptability:**

Play builds resilience by encouraging a mindset that embraces failure as a learning opportunity. Leaders who play are more adaptable and able to bounce back from setbacks, turning challenges into opportunities for growth.

The Magic of Play

Play is an act of the imagination—it's dreaming at work. When you watch children actively playing, what do you observe? You see pure creativity in motion. They dream out loud, turning simple objects into magical things. They solve problems, create worlds, and learn without any limitations. Now, think about adults at play. It might not be as obvious, but when we let ourselves play, we open up the same door to imagination. We dream big, problem-solve creatively, and find solutions we didn't even know we were capable of.

This book is a perfect setting for us to practice our craft as leaders who believe in the power of play. Pay attention to those moments when you feel your imagination at work and your dreams coming to life. I'll start by sharing one of mine: growing up in a house full of strife, I saw some pretty ugly things. My father was a drug addict, my mother was a teenage mom with learning disabilities, and sometimes it felt like the world was caving in. But play was my escape. My brother and I would create costumes, build props, make up songs, and disappear into our own world for hours.

That's when I learned that play was the antidote to fear and sadness. As I grew older and had children of my own, I wanted nothing to do with the world I grew up in. I wanted to facilitate play for my children as much as possible to create an entirely different reality for them. I started my school with that same passion for play.

But as the responsibilities piled up, as life got busier and heavier, I—like so many of us—forgot to play. I let the "joy vampires" creep in. It took that idea for this book to remind me of what I had lost. I made a commitment to put play back in my life, and it changed everything. That decision to prioritize play made me a better mom, teacher, leader, and person.

Play and Mental Health: My Passion for Change

We live in a heavy world, and mental health is at the center of it all—both for kids and adults. I've seen the impact of play on mental health up close with my daughter, Abbie. She's struggled with anxiety her whole life and is on the autism spectrum, but play has been her lifeline. She now runs our entire school-age program, and I've watched her tap into play to bring joy back into her life. She'll say, "Mom, I forgot to play," and it's a reminder to all of us. When she plays, she's recharged and ready to take on the world.

Play isn't just about having fun. It's about healing, energizing, and connecting. Research shows that play helps teachers manage stress, avoid burnout, and stay connected to the deeper meaning of their work. It gives them hope and brings back the joy of teaching. And it's the same for leaders. If we're not playing, we're not tapping into the creative energy that keeps us going.

The Seven Principles of Self-Active Play for Adults

1. CREATIVE ENERGY: Play generates creative energy and revitalizes the human spirit.

2. HANDS-ON PLAY: Open-ended, hands-on activities reconnect us with earlier stages of life, evoking deep emotions like hope and purpose.

3. PLAY SPACE: The play space is self-constructed and based on feelings of safety and trust.

4. PROTECTIVENESS & CURIOSITY: Play spaces elicit strong emotional responses, like a desire to protect or return to them for further exploration.

5. PRETEND ROLES: As adults take on new pretend roles during play, they explore "what will happen next" with excitement.

6. CONNECTION WITH OTHERS: Play fosters strong connections with others, and the positive feelings extend beyond the play space.

7. INTUITIVE SELF: Play lets adults experience spontaneity of the spirit and trust their inner selves.

My MAGIC Framework for Playful Leadership

I've developed a framework called MAGIC to help you become a Practically Perfect PLAYFUL Leader. Here's what MAGIC stands for:

M: Mastering Mindset

Your mindset is the foundation of your leadership. If you and your team don't have the right mindset, growth is impossible. Everything starts here.

A: Assessing the Pain Points

You need to be brutally honest about where the pain points are—in yourself, your team, and your business. Identify the gaps, and then focus on attacking them first.

G: Grounded for Growth

To grow, you need to stay grounded. Take care of your own needs—mentally, physically, and emotionally—so you can care for your team and your business.

I: Influence

Your influence is your power to get people on board. You can't grow without sharing your vision, inspiring others, and getting people excited to come along on the journey with you.

C: Clarity and Capacity

You can't have one without the other. Clarity shows you where the walls are, and capacity is what you need to build to keep growing. You have to teach other leaders how to build capacity too, so they can take your vision and expand it even further.

By embracing play and the MAGIC framework, you'll find that leadership becomes less about struggle and more about creativity, collaboration, and joy. Together, we can build environments where people thrive, where creativity flows, and where everyone, from children to leaders, learn how to play again.

APPLICATION QUESTIONS

☐ Think about a time when play helped you break through a leadership challenge. What lessons did you learn, and how can you apply them moving forward?

☐ In what ways do you see play as essential to preventing burnout, both for you as a leader and for your team?

☐ How can you implement more structured playtime or playful elements into your team's daily routine to foster a more resilient and engaged workforce?

CHAPTER 2

(M) MASTER YOUR MINDSET AND PREPARE FOR "A TWISTER ON THE HORIZON"

It doesn't matter how much training, education and experience you have, if you fail to master your mindset as a leader, you will fail to lead. I have personally had to work for years on mastering my mindset. The fact that I have ADHD makes me extremely impulsive, and I am also very empathetic and an empath. I have learned to recognize my triggers and use them to fuel my growth instead of hindering it.

In *The Wizard of Oz*, the twister that sweeps Dorothy away from Kansas to the magical land of Oz symbolizes sudden and unexpected change. Just like her twister, leaders often face unknown challenges that can disrupt their plans and require quick adaptation.

In order to prepare for a twister on the horizon, we must embrace positivity.

Dorothy's journey begins with a twister, a chaotic event that uproots her life. Instead of succumbing to fear and despair, she embraces the adventure with a positive attitude. Leaders can learn to view unexpected challenges and chaos as opportunities for growth and new experiences, maintaining a constructive outlook even when faced with adversity. Embracing positivity, however, does not mean being blind to challenges or having a toxic positive attitude where you just throw sparkles on everything and call it good.

Positivity is only part of the journey as we must also develop resilience along our path toward leadership excellence. Throughout her journey, Dorothy encounters numerous obstacles, from wicked witches to complex paths. Her resilience keeps her moving forward. Similarly, leaders must develop the ability to bounce back from setbacks, viewing failures as stepping stones rather than end points. The more challenges we face, the more we rewire the pathways in our brain to become more resilient. This resilience is crucial for navigating through the "twisters" of leadership.

"Leadership is not about being unflappable; it's about knowing how to recover when you are. Resilient leaders rise not because they avoid the storm, but because they weather it with grace and fortitude."
—SHERYL SANDBERG

With resilience comes flexibility, which is an invaluable trait as a leader. The *Yellow Brick Road* is not a straight path, and Dorothy must adapt to changing circumstances and new companions along the way. Flexibility allows her to find alternative solutions and continue her journey, and for her to discover that those companions ultimately turn out to be her champions. If you are too closed-minded and inflexible to collaborate and learn from others, you will be missing out on special learning opportunities. Leaders, too, must be adaptable, ready to pivot strategies, be innovative, and embrace new ideas when the situation demands it.

Due to my father's drug and alcohol addictions, my mother made the heart-wrenching decision to leave him. I was left with a swirl of confusion and heartache. Despite his struggles, I always looked forward to seeing him, clinging to the hope that each promise he made would be kept.

I remember so vividly those many times I sat on the curb, waiting for him to come pick me up. The excitement of seeing him would build inside me, only to be extinguished as the hours ticked by and he never showed up. These memories actually make me feel the heaviness in my heart, and I never want my children to experience that type of abandonment and pain. Each time he forgot about me, my heart would shatter a little more, but it also taught me a harsh truth about life's unpredictability. These moments, as painful as they were, began to instill in me a deep sense of patience and emotional resilience that would later become my strength.

Adding to these challenges, I had dyslexia and ADHD at a time when society and the education system knew little about these conditions. School became a battleground where I fought to keep up with my peers, often feeling lost and frustrated. Math was especially torturous, each math problem a mountain to climb. I faced constant struggles with concentration and staying on task. I often felt like I wasn't good enough and I never would be. In third grade, there was a bulletin board with stars on it for all the kids with star-studded cursive. I went through the whole school year and never made it to the star board, and I wanted so desperately to be a star. This didn't just affect my academics; it seeped into my social life, making me feel different and isolated from my classmates.

As I grew older, these experiences profoundly shaped me. They gave me a deep understanding of adversity and the importance of support and perseverance. I learned the value of empathy from my personal struggles, using this understanding to connect with others who faced their own challenges. My journey from a little girl waiting on the curb for a father who often didn't show up, to an adult who faced and overcame significant educational and social hurdles, is a testament to my incredible resilience.

Now, as a leader, I bring a unique perspective shaped by my past. I understand the pain of being forgotten, the frustration of being misunderstood, and the inner strength it takes to keep going.

My mom was a teen mom, and even so, she recognized she was not able to give us the same kind of home environment her own mother, our grandma, provided. We did not live in the pretty house where everything always seemed perfect, clean, and organized. To this day, my mother strives to make up for the fact she was not the homemaker my grandma is. My brother and I gravitated to Grandma, so Mom went at things in a different way.

She was a teenager when she married Dad, who was already addicted to drugs and alcohol. Things were not easy and far from perfect, so she found a way to make up for the shortcomings. Mom had a knack for making everything magical and she still does. Even though she had little to no money, she would come up with crazy ways to make special occasions super special, especially our birthdays. For example, when I was in third grade, she made my birthday a 50s theme. She found old 45s and records and hung them on the walls. We had 50s music playing to dance to, and she made my friends and I costumes to wear. She always went above and beyond when she could. When I was growing up, it seemed that she became the event person when anyone was planning occasions and events. Despite the fact that she didn't even have a high school diploma, she got a job in a company starting out as a secretary. In time, she worked her way up the ladder to become the number two person in the company and planned all their events. Now, she plans all my events for my company. She took her passion to provide joy and magic and made it part of her life's work.

I didn't realize until I had kids of my own that I do this exact thing for my own family. All the holiday celebrations are at our house, and we go overboard to make holidays unforgettable. Now, I do this in my company. At the schools, even when onboarding a new staff member and with our mentor programs, we make everything fun and magical. I'll ask my team to come up with ideas, and then tell them, "Now, come back to me and make it magical." I want them to make the extra effort to bring shock and awe to our students and families.

It doesn't always take money to do what my mom did for us, and you can do that for others. Mom is into nature. She's a journey person, where I am a destination person. Mom teaches me to slow down and see what I might be missing. She takes long walks and rides her horse into the wilderness. She enjoys the journey and the process to get there. She teaches me to look around and learn to be part of the process myself, not just arrive at the destination. Don't miss the little things along the way. That too is part of how to make things magical.

We change the environment of the classrooms every two to three weeks. The teachers give me their lesson plans and what they hope to accomplish. I want them to set the stage to engage, so that kids and parents are enthralled like they are at Disney when they walk into their classrooms. I ask the teachers to get down on their students' level and see, feel, and smell things like they would. I want them to know how the kids will experience what they've created. What questions will they ask? What will create a sense of wonder?

For example, if they are going to study bugs, think like the classroom reflects the movie, *Honey, I Shrunk the Kids*. Use things we have and make it feel like the kids are the bugs. Use big sheets of green paper to make giant blades of grass, pool noodles to make flower stems with paper flower petals, and fake dirt for a digging area. Make them feel like they are part of the environment, seeing things from the bugs' perspective. I think that will make them understand more about bugs than simply reading about them in books.

Innovation is part of what creates the magic, and it can be accomplished by optimizing what we currently have and reusing things. The schools have tons of resources. They can also use videos and projections. In the case of the bugs, they can use giant images to reinforce the feeling of being a tiny bug.

If you are in leadership in a corporate environment or factory, you can do similar things. Just think out of the box. Retaining staff is easier when there is fun and magic. Staff retention is a big issue for a lot of companies. It's imperative to have a play first mindset. Everyone needs play in their life. We do a staff potluck every month, and we make it a dress up event. We did one where we had them dress as a dream they have for themselves. One teacher dressed up as a passport because they want to travel; another as a race car driver. They each brought their favorite dish to share.

Potlucks are easy to do. It can be a lunch potluck where people bring a dish that represents their culture. Have a daily dance break. Blare a song throughout the building and encourage staff to just loosen up, stop work, and dance for three to five minutes. Stop everything and everyone dances. This can work in the back of the house at restaurants or hotels, real estate offices, or factories. All kinds of environments can do this kind of thing. Food, music, and dance can bring the magic.

We do a weekly staff appreciation event. Directors have a budget, and we plan it out for the entire year. It's important to make it magical and memorable. Disney says you can change someone's day in less than five minutes if you make it magical. When you do these things, it spreads to everyone in the lives of your staff, their kids, parents, and community. It can't be contained, and you will spread the magic like wildfire before you know it.

Our emotions are our data; it is up to us to figure out how to use them!

One of the most powerful examples of mastering mindset comes from my own family. Both of my boys play football, and they've had to work hard to keep their heads in the game. My son Zack suffered a major injury that could have ended his athletic career. He could have let that injury defeat him, but instead, he chose a different path. He didn't give up/ He asked questions, worked with experts, nutritionists, and trainers, and did everything in his power to come back stronger. But just when he was able to return to the field, he blew out his arm, breaking it in three places. That officially ended his football career.

Watching my son face this devastating reality was heartbreaking, but what I witnessed was nothing short of remarkable. Zack mastered his mindset. Instead of letting the end of his football career defeat him, he shifted his energy into helping others. He took all the hard work, discipline, and mindset training he had built over the years and redirected it into his next steps, using his experience to lift others up. That's what mastering mindset looks like in action. It's taking your pain, your setbacks, and your disappointments, and turning them into opportunities to grow, to lead, and to serve others.

Leadership and the Athlete's Mindset

Athletes like Zack, along with their coaches, constantly work on mastering their mindset. It's not just about physical strength or technical skill, but mental resilience, focus, and adaptability. Coaches use specific strategies to help athletes stay mentally tough, and these same strategies can be applied to leadership.

One common tool athletes use is visualization. Before stepping onto the field, many athletes mentally rehearse the game, seeing themselves succeed in their mind's eye. This practice prepares them for what's ahead, allowing them to perform at their best even under pressure. As leaders, we can apply the same technique. Visualization helps us mentally prepare for important decisions, challenging conversations, and even unexpected crises. By visualizing success, we can train our brains to stay focused and confident, even in difficult situations.

Athletes and their coaches also focus heavily on goal setting—both short-term and long-term. This keeps them focused, motivated, and always working toward a larger objective. Breaking down big dreams into smaller, more manageable goals is key to staying on track. In leadership, this is just as important. We need to set clear, measurable goals not only for ourselves but also for our teams. This practice not only provides direction but also gives people a sense of accomplishment as they hit those milestones.

Lastly, a crucial part of an athlete's mindset is embracing failure as part of the process. No one wins every time, and the best athletes understand that setbacks are inevitable. What matters is how you bounce back. This principle applies directly to leadership. There will be moments when you fail or when things don't go as planned. Leaders who master their mindset know how to recover, learn, and move forward stronger than before.

The Role of Mindset in Mental Health

The connection between mindset and mental health is undeniable. Mental health issues such as anxiety, depression, and burnout are rampant, especially in today's fast-paced, high-pressure work environments. Leaders who focus on mastering their mindset are better equipped to handle these challenges, both for themselves and for their teams.

Research shows that maintaining a growth mindset—the belief that abilities and intelligence can be developed through dedication and hard work—has a profound effect on mental health. Leaders with a growth mindset view challenges not as threats but as opportunities to learn and grow. This perspective reduces stress, fosters resilience, and encourages continuous improvement, which is crucial in preventing burnout.

Leaders can model this growth mindset for their teams, creating an environment where mistakes are seen as learning opportunities, and success is measured not just by outcomes but by effort and growth. This not only boosts morale but also helps team members build their own mental resilience.

When it comes to mental health, play is a powerful tool for maintaining balance. Play isn't just for kids—it's for adults, too. In fact, play has been proven to reduce stress, increase creativity, and improve overall mental well-being. When leaders incorporate play into the workplace—whether through team-building activities, creative brainstorming sessions, or even lighthearted competitions—they create a more positive, engaging work environment. This leads to lower stress levels, higher job satisfaction, and, ultimately, better mental health for everyone involved.

Athletes know this well. Even in the most intense training regimens, there are moments of play. Whether it's a friendly game of soccer after a grueling practice or a fun team-building exercise, athletes use play to relieve tension, build camaraderie, and reignite their passion for the sport. Leaders can do the same for their teams.

Cultivating a Culture of Resilience

Mastering your mindset as a leader goes beyond personal growth—it extends to your entire team. When leaders focus on their own mindset, they set the tone for the rest of the organization. A leader who models resilience, positivity, and adaptability can inspire their team to do the same.

One powerful way to cultivate this culture is by encouraging open communication and vulnerability. Create a space where team members feel comfortable sharing their struggles, setbacks, and challenges without fear of judgment. This not only builds trust but also allows the team to work together to find solutions.

Additionally, leaders can provide tools and resources to help their teams master their own mindsets. Whether it's offering professional development opportunities, bringing in mental health experts, or simply encouraging regular breaks for play and relaxation, leaders who prioritize their team's mental well-being create a more engaged, productive, and innovative workforce.

Mastering mindset is a continuous process. Just like athletes, we must train our minds daily, push through the discomfort, and learn to adapt. As leaders, our role is not just to lead by example, but to create an environment where our team can thrive mentally and emotionally.

APPLICATION QUESTIONS

1. Identify Your Mindset Triggers:

☐ What are some situations that commonly trigger negative thoughts or impulsive behaviors for you? How can you recognize these triggers earlier?

☐ Reflect on a recent situation where you allowed your emotions to guide your actions. What mindset strategies could you have employed to shift your perspective and respond differently?

2. Developing Resilience Through Setbacks:

☐ Think about a major setback you've faced (personally or professionally). How did you initially react? In hindsight, how could you have used this experience to build resilience?

☐ In the story about Zack's injury, he didn't give up after his setbacks but instead channeled his energy into helping others. How can you apply a similar mindset to challenges you are currently facing?

☐ What practices or habits can you implement to build greater resilience in yourself and your team?

3. Embrace Flexibility in Leadership:

☐ Leaders, like Dorothy on the Yellow Brick Road, must adapt to changing circumstances. Can you recall a time when you needed to pivot or adjust your leadership approach? What did you learn from that experience?

☐ Flexibility often means learning from unexpected sources. How can you encourage collaboration and openness within your team to benefit from diverse perspectives and approaches?

4. Strengthening Emotional Intelligence:

☐ As a leader, how do you practice empathy when managing your team? Do you find it challenging to balance empathy with decisiveness? What can you do to improve your emotional intelligence?

☐ Think about a situation where you misunderstood someone's emotions or perspective. How could better emotional awareness have changed the outcome?

5. Mindset Mastery for Leaders:

☐ Mastering mindset often requires a clear vision and goals. How do you ensure you stay grounded and focused on your long-term objectives, even when facing challenges or stress?

☐ Zack's story highlights the importance of seeking expert advice and focusing on self-improvement. How do you seek out guidance or mentorship when you're struggling with your own mindset as a leader?

6. Application to Your Team's Mental Health:

☐ Mental health challenges can deeply impact team performance and morale. How can you, as a leader, foster an environment that encourages open communication about mental health and supports individuals in need?

☐ How can you introduce play into your work culture to combat stress, improve morale, and promote mental well-being among your team members?

7. Play as a Mindset Tool:

☐ In this book, play is presented as a solution for burnout and low morale. Think of a time when you or your team felt overwhelmed. How could incorporating play have shifted the energy or mindset of the group?

☐ How can you implement small, playful activities in your daily leadership practice to reduce stress and enhance your team's creative problem-solving?

8. Action Plan for Mastering Your Mindset:

☐ Based on what you've learned in this chapter, what are the key areas of mindset mastery you need to focus on to improve your leadership?

☐ What practical steps can you take this week to strengthen your mindset, both personally and as a leader?

9. Magic and Inspiration:

☐ How has the concept of "magic," or creating magical moments influenced your leadership approach? Can you share a specific example where this mindset helped you lead effectively?

☐ Reflect on how magical events have inspired you. How can you incorporate this sense of magic into your leadership to inspire and uplift your team?

CHAPTER 3:

IS LEADERSHIP FOR YOU?

It's kind of a yes-or-no question.

It's okay to ask yourself this question, and it's equally okay if the answer is a resounding no! Not everyone needs to be a leader, and in fact, that's a very good thing. Someone has to follow; in fact, a lot of people do, or the world would grind to a halt. Whether you call it God or the universe, you will eventually know if leadership is your calling, and you'll seek leadership if you're pulled to it.

You might be wondering why I chose the story of *The Wizard of Oz* and the journey down that iconic path and what it has to do with leadership. Let's explore the symbolism of the *Yellow Brick Road*. As you continue reading, you'll discover several reasons I relate my entrepreneurial journey to Dorothy's path. Initially, what made this connection clear to me was the imagery of the *Yellow Brick Road* leading to something grandiose and spectacular, serving as a metaphor for gaining answers and perspective on life. What later stood out, however, was not the destination but the journey itself, marked by discovery and the characters Dorothy encountered who became her champions. Dorothy learned a lot about herself each step of the way, and her new friends were the catalyst for most of that learning.

My love for the topic of leadership stems from the champions in my own life who have shaped who I am today, and now I am fortunate to be someone else's champion.

My Story of Leadership and Family Champions

My mom was just 16 years old when she had me. She was still living with my maternal grandparents at the time. My grandma and grandpa helped support her until she married my dad. I don't remember exactly when she moved out, but I do remember her and my dad living in an apartment together when I was very young. My brother was born two years after I was, and he had bronchitis and other breathing issues, so it seemed like he was often ill. There were several times when my mom made us leave my father. She would always say, "Your dad is making your brother sick," and I remember feeling sad and confused whenever we would have to leave. I can still picture the car parked out in front of the apartment and wondering why we had to leave. Why was my dad making my brother sick?

There were other times when it felt as if there was a dark cloud hanging over the living room. I vividly remember seeing some type of drugs splayed out on the coffee table there. I couldn't tell you what type of drugs. There was alcohol on the table too, and people were always hanging around the apartment. To this day, if I watch any kind of movie or am around any type of situation where there's any kind of visible drugs, I have vivid flashbacks of my early childhood, and the sadness and confusion seep back in.

Living in that situation made me latch onto my grandparents even more, because whenever we went to their house, I would feel happy. They had a lovely place where my brother and I always felt safe. There was never any talk about making my brother sick, and there were never random people coming and going. The dark cloud I saw in my own home never existed there. They were always just my happy, safe place. My grandma always had food cooking, and the rich smells filled the air in her kitchen. She would carefully set the table with pretty plates and cups for the meals and made things so beautiful. I knew early on this was something that I wanted to have and how I wanted to live. I craved that stability, the beauty in the environment, and being taken care of—but I also wanted to take care of my brother. He was still often sick, which created an underlying desire to take care of him. I think that desire stemmed from my grandma because she made me feel so taken care of and so safe. I wanted to give that same feeling to my brother.

I didn't realize until much later in life how much her leadership as a caretaker affected me and how much of an impact that had on my life. All I knew was I wanted to become a mother and caretaker, and later, a teacher. All of this translated into me becoming a leader. I strove to take care of the people leading my schools, making sure the teachers were well taken care of—meaning that ultimately, the children were well taken care of. That all reflects back on my grandma. She was my very first example of what it takes to be a leader. I don't think she knows how powerful of an impact she had on my life and what a great leader she was, and is, to this day.

The Courage to Lead: An Inheritance

Leadership and the courage to lead come in many different forms, some you might not even think of as leadership roles. My grandma is the leader of our entire family, even though she doesn't see herself as a leader. If you asked her if she's a leader or if she wants to be a leader, she would probably say no. But I don't agree. To me, she will always be a leader.

My grandpa was also one of the best leaders I have ever known, as well as being one of the best humans I have ever known. He led many teams and organizations, and despite never being a wealthy man, his personality was magnetic. People wanted to follow him. He was one of the kindest people that ever walked this earth, and he had brilliant ideas. He was funny, and his smile was contagious.

Now that he has passed away, my grandma felt she could admit that she believes she doesn't have the charisma, power, and influence that he had. But that's so not true. My grandma led her family from day one. She always wanted our family to be well taken care of, loved, prayed for, and thought well of. She was the one I always went to when I needed anything—from advice to encouragement. Her silent courage to lead really stood out. She had the courage to always pray for her family and be the glue that held us together, even when it was seemingly falling apart. And when there were people in our family who were harder to love, my grandma was the one who was leading with love, consistency, and her calming nature.

Her form of leadership stood out to me from the time I was very young. As a leader, she was (and still is) somebody that I wanted to emulate. She was beautiful. She is beautiful, and she is still leading with love, always there, always consistent. I want to be around her as much as possible, and I think that having the courage to lead your family is something that is not talked about enough. It inspires me every day to be a leader for my family.

When you have the courage to lead your family, even in uncertain times, and the courage to show up when nobody else can or will, it plants a seed in your children to become future leaders. That's what my grandma did for me. I wanted to be like my grandma when I grew up, and I didn't know what that meant at the time. I just knew that she was somebody I looked up to, somebody I admired. To this day, whenever I'm writing or preparing for a speech or creating curriculum, she's the first person I think of, and I want her opinion. I want her feedback because she's such an incredible silent leader. She does the research, and she does the homework, always quietly leading.

A Journey of Influence

One of those early champions I encountered indirectly was John Maxwell. As a teenager, I was on the cheer squad with his daughter and niece at Christian High School in San Diego. At the time, I had no idea who John Maxwell was or the kind of leadership impact he would eventually have on the world. To me, he was simply the pastor of Skyline Church, leading a congregation with incredible influence, energy, and passion. But even then, as young as I was, I felt there was something different about him. He had this magnetic presence that drew people in. Everyone wanted to follow him, learn from him, and grow under his leadership.

Maxwell started at Skyline Church, but his leadership journey didn't stop there. He became one of the most influential thought leaders in the world of leadership development. His books, seminars, and teachings, such as, *The 21 Irrefutable Laws of Leadership* and *Developing the Leader Within You*, have impacted millions globally. One of his quotes that always resonated with me is:

> *"A leader is one who knows the way,*
> *goes the way, and shows the way."*
> —JOHN C. MAXWELL

I saw Maxwell's leadership in action firsthand at Skyline Church. The way he communicated with clarity, the way he drew people to him, and the way he empowered others made an impression on me, even though I didn't fully grasp the depth of his influence at the time. Watching him lead with such conviction and purpose lit a spark in me. While I didn't know it then, that spark would later grow into a desire to lead others, to inspire change, and to nurture growth in those around me.

What Makes John Maxwell and Other Great Leaders Stand Out

The qualities that make John Maxwell a great leader are qualities any of us can develop with the right mindset and determination. Here are some of the key attributes I believe make Maxwell, and other great leaders, stand out:

1. **Vision:** Maxwell has always had a clear vision of where he's going and what he wants to accomplish. He communicates that vision clearly and inspires others to rally around it. As he says, "A leader's job is not to put greatness into people, but to recognize that it already exists, and to help them see it for themselves."

2. **Communication:** A hallmark of Maxwell's leadership is his ability to communicate effectively. Great leaders are great communicators. They can articulate their vision and motivate others to take action. This is a skill I've worked hard to develop in my own leadership journey.

3. **Empathy:** As a pastor, Maxwell deeply understood the importance of empathy in leadership. He could connect with his congregation because he genuinely cared about their well-being.

Leaders who prioritize empathy create a culture of trust and loyalty, which is essential for long-term success.

4. **Influence:** Maxwell teaches that leadership is influence—nothing more, nothing less. It's not about power or authority; it's about how you make others feel and what kind of impact you have on their lives. This is a core principle I've embraced in my own leadership philosophy.

5. **Servant Leadership:** Great leaders, like Maxwell, understand that leadership is about serving others. It's about putting the needs of your team ahead of your own and making sure they have what they need to succeed. Maxwell embodies this philosophy, and it's something I've tried to emulate in my own work.

6. **Resilience:** Leadership comes with its fair share of challenges and setbacks. One of the most important traits of a great leader is resilience—the ability to bounce back from adversity and keep moving forward. Maxwell's leadership journey, from starting as a small church pastor to becoming a global leadership expert, is a testament to this quality.

Maxwell has a special gift for influencing others, and it comes from his ability to connect with people on a deep level. He talks about how leadership is not about titles, positions, or flowcharts—it's about one life influencing another. His emphasis on relationships and servant leadership is a cornerstone of his teaching:

"People don't care how much you know until they know how much you care."
— JOHN C. MAXWELL

As I reflect on my leadership journey, I realize that the seeds were planted back in those days of watching Maxwell lead his congregation. He was a leader people wanted to follow, and that's one of the most important qualities of any leader—being the kind of person that others want to follow because they trust you, they believe in your vision, and they know you care.

Action Items for Aspiring Leaders

- [ ] **Reflect on Your Vision:** What is your vision for your life and leadership? How can you clearly communicate that vision to inspire others?

- [ ] **Practice Empathy:** Think about a time when you led with empathy. How did it affect your team or those around you? What steps can you take to improve your empathetic leadership?

- [ ] **Focus on Influence:** Consider who you influence in your day-to-day life. How can you use that influence to positively impact those around you?

- [ ] **Embrace Resilience:** Reflect on a time when you faced a leadership challenge. How did you bounce back?

- [ ] What lessons did you learn that you can apply to future challenges?

Remember, leadership is a journey, and the best leaders are those who are always learning, growing, and striving to be better for the people they serve.

Whether you feel called to leadership or you're still exploring that path, remember that great leadership is about growth, humility, and a desire to serve. The journey may not always be easy, and there will be many "twisters" along the way, but if you master your mindset, embrace the influence you have on others, and lead with empathy and vision, you can become the kind of leader people want to follow.

CHAPTER 4:

(A) ASSESSING THE PAIN POINTS

*"For a man to conquer himself is the
first and noblest of all victories."*
—Plato

Y ou have to be able to assess yourself as a leader and assess
the issues faced by the members of your team. If you
can't see your own flaws, problems, and issues, you can't
help your team see and work on theirs. We all have triggers, things
that may send us into a tailspin. We all have things we aren't good
at. Do you have issues with learning new technologies? Are you
weak or strong when it comes to organization? Do you get angry
or frustrated when you need help with something? Whatever you
deal with, you have to learn to move through the problem or train
someone else to take on the task or deal with those issues. This is
where having a strong and well-trained staff comes in. But first,
you need to assess where the problems are, where the strengths
lie, and who has the strongest and weakest skills in each area of

concern or each task at hand. I have created a tool for my staff, and perhaps, it will help you to assess your pain points and strengths and that of your staff.

To become a truly great leader, you have to have extreme emotional intelligence and learn to embrace self-reflection. These are learnable skills. You can begin by looking at yourself in earnest, seeing the gaps and the strengths and accept them. You may have imposter syndrome, but assessment will help you see things in a clearer light. Knowing your gaps is just an opportunity for growth as a leader.

This assessment tool can be revisited as often as needed. In my opinion, we should reevaluate our pain points and strengths at least once or twice a year as noted below. Things change rapidly in my industry and the same can be said for most businesses.

Mindset Goals

This worksheet will help you identify the root problem behind your goals and chart a path forward. Write down each goal you want to achieve, the reason why it is important to you, and the measurable outcome.

Area I struggle

WHY I STRUGGLE	MEASURABLE OUTCOME

Area I am strong

WHY AM I STRONG	MEASURABLE OUTCOME

Area I am improving

WHY AM I IMPROVING	MEASURABLE OUTCOME

Achieving Goals

What are my short-term goals?

_____
_____
_____
_____

Why do I want to achieve them?

_____
_____
_____
_____

What habits do I need to keep in order to achieve them?

_____
_____
_____
_____

What habits might slow me down in achieving them?

_____
_____
_____
_____

Escaping My Comfort Zone

Why am I afraid of leaving my comfort zone?

_____

_____

_____

_____

How can I overcome my fear of leaving my comfort zone?

_____

_____

_____

_____

What will happen if I stay in my comfort zone?

_____

_____

_____

_____

What will my life look like after I leave my comfort zone?

_____

_____

_____

_____

Weekly Review

What have I been focusing on this week?
_____
_____

What actions have I taken this week?
_____
_____

What accomplishments have I had?
_____
_____

What challenges did I face?
_____
_____

How many time audits did I do?
_____
_____

What have I learned this week?
_____
_____

How do I feel about my progress this week?
_____
_____

Discovery Kidzone Leadership Pain Point and Strength Diagnostic Tool

Step 1: Launch a Pulse Survey

- **Frequency:** Conduct this survey quarterly or at least annually.
- **Method:** Use an anonymous survey platform.

Survey Questions:

What should the organization/team keep doing?

_____

_____

_____

_____

What should the organization/team stop doing?

_____

_____

_____

_____

What should the organization/team start doing?

_____

_____

_____

_____

How aligned do you feel with the company's purpose and values?

_____

_____

_____

_____

How do you perceive the team's current goals and strategies?

_____

_____

_____

_____

Do you feel empowered by the company's structure and tactics to do your job effectively?

_____

_____

_____

_____

Are the current metrics and outcomes clear and achievable?

_____

_____

_____

_____

Step 2: Gather External Feedback

- **Customer Experience Data:** Use Net Promoter Scores (NPS) to get a broad sense of customer satisfaction, but pair it with:

- **Mystery Shopping:** To observe staff interactions and service delivery.

- **Online Reviews Analysis:** Identify recurring themes and perceptions in reviews.

- **Focus Groups:** Conduct focus groups with parents to gather deeper insights into their satisfaction.

Step 3: Executive Team Review

- Collaborate with the leadership team to analyze the gathered data (both internal and external).

- **Plot Data on the Performance Matrix:** Use the following four areas to identify where the team is experiencing alignment or misalignment:

1. Purpose & Values:

- Does the team understand and align with the core values and mission?

- Do they feel their work is meaningful?

2. Strategy & Goals:

- Are goals clear and actionable?

- Does the team feel like they are on the path to achieving these goals?

3. *Structure & Tactics*:

- Is the organizational structure supportive of day-to-day tasks?
- Are there clear tactics or processes that help team members do their jobs?

4. *Metrics & Outcomes*:

- Are metrics fair and measurable?
- Is the team motivated to meet or exceed these outcomes?

Step 4: Analyze for Misalignment

- **Identifying Pain Points:** Once the data is plotted, look for areas of misalignment.

  Common pain points may include:

  - Lack of clarity in roles and goals (Strategy & Goals misalignment).
  - Insufficient resources or ineffective systems (Structure & Tactics misalignment).
  - Inconsistent or unclear performance metrics (Metrics & Outcomes misalignment).
  - Disengagement or lack of buy-in to company values (Purpose & Values misalignment).

Step 5: Prioritize Pain Points

- **Severity & Impact:** Prioritize pain points based on how much they affect the team's performance.

- **Feasibility:** Consider which issues can be solved in the short term and which require long-term strategies.

Step 6: Root Cause Analysis

- **Go deeper:** For each pain point, investigate its root cause. *Example: If "Metrics & Outcomes" is a pain point, is it due to a lack of clear communication or unrealistic expectations?*

Step 7: Action Planning

- **Assign Responsibilities:** Designate leaders to tackle specific areas of misalignment.

- **Create an Action Plan:** Break down solutions into actionable steps with timelines.

Step 8: Continuous Improvement

- **Ongoing Monitoring:** Implement follow-up surveys to track progress.

- **Adjust Strategies:** Be flexible and adjust plans based on ongoing feedback and data analysis.

- **Situational Leadership Integration:** Use the Situational Leadership Model to adapt your leadership approach based on the identified pain points:

- **Directing:** If your team lacks clarity (e.g., in Structure & Tactics), you may need to provide more specific instructions and guidance.

- **Coaching:** When a team understands the goals but needs support, provide motivation and encouragement.

- **Supporting:** When your team is competent but perhaps unmotivated or disengaged, offer emotional support and recognition.

- **Delegating:** For high-performing and self-sufficient teams, empower them to take more initiative while still monitoring alignment with overall goals.

Some Key Elements of Leadership – Communication and Operation:

There's a difference between being a good leader and being a good communicator and/or a good operator. While being a good communicator and a good operator are essential skills, they do not necessarily make someone a great leader. Here's why:

The Good Communicator: They can articulate ideas clearly, listen actively, and engage in meaningful dialogue, but without vision and inspiration, communication alone won't motivate a team to achieve greatness.

Good Operator: They can manage processes efficiently and ensure tasks are completed on time, but without empathy and adaptability, operational excellence alone won't inspire loyalty or innovation.

Honestly, the term, "good operator," still makes me laugh out loud. When I started my business, I was the absolute worst operator you could imagine! God must've had a big plan for me and my company because, let me tell you, I was not it at the time. I didn't even know what systems or processes were—I was flying by the seat of my pants every single day! I didn't keep records, and I'm not sure I even had a file cabinet. It was embarrassing, to say the least.

I look back and cringe, wondering how in the world we made it through those early days. My idea of "operations" was just hoping everything would somehow fall into place. Spoiler alert: it didn't. I was constantly putting out fires that could have been avoided if I had even the slightest clue about creating systems or managing efficiently. It took years—literal years—of blood, sweat, tears, and countless mistakes before I finally started getting it right. Every time I thought we were on the right track, I'd realize, nope, we're still flying blind here.

What I eventually figured out was that the biggest pain point in the business wasn't a lack of systems or processes—it was me. I was the bottleneck, and that was a tough pill to swallow. I had to face the fact that I couldn't do it all on my own, and more importantly, I wasn't supposed to. I needed people who were smarter, more organized, and, let's be real, more operationally-minded than me to help carry the vision forward.

Fast forward a bit, and the business was growing fast. We had an incredible team in place, and I finally felt like we were on the verge of something huge. But old habits die hard, and I found myself slipping back into that operational role. Somehow, I ended up doing most of the backend stuff myself again. And if you remember anything from my earlier story, you'll know—me handling operations is a bad idea! I had to stop and assess the situation, and that's when it hit me again: "Hi, I'm the problem, it's me!" I was holding us back by trying to wear too many hats, and it wasn't sustainable.

That's when I knew it was time to bring in someone who could not only do the job, but excel at it. Enter Jen G—my number two, my rock, the yin to my yang. Jen is everything I'm not when it comes to operations. She is organized, methodical, and has this magical ability to take chaos and turn it into a well-oiled machine. Hiring her was a scary financial risk at the time, but looking back, it was one of the best decisions I've ever made. The peace of mind she brings, knowing that the operational side of things is handled with precision and care, is priceless.

The lesson here? When you're evaluating the pain points in your business, don't just look at the systems or the team—take a good, hard look at yourself. Are you the bottleneck? Are you trying to do too much or do things you're not great at? And more importantly, are you willing to bring in people who are better than you at the things you struggle with? Because that's what leadership is about. It's not about doing everything yourself—it's about building a team that fills in your gaps and helps bring your vision to life.

In the end, the best operators aren't necessarily the ones who do it all themselves. They're the ones who know when to step back, admit "I'm the problem," trust their team, and focus on the bigger picture.

What It Takes to Be a Great Leader:

1. Visionary Thinking:

Big Picture Focus: A great leader sees beyond the immediate tasks and goals, understanding the broader mission and long-term objectives of the business or organization. This is not to say they don't have attention to detail, but they don't get bogged down in the minutia so much they cannot make the big plans and dreams happen. It's a matter of seeing all of it from the small goals to the big wins.

Inspiration: Leaders can articulate a compelling vision that inspires, influences, and motivates others to contribute to a shared goal. Great leaders are both inspiring and inspired. They are excited about new ideas and innovations. They want to learn constantly and teach others about what they learn as they go. People follow leaders that make them feel something, that move them to act.

In thinking about what it takes to be a great leader, I believe the most important element of a leader is visionary thinking. A great leader takes a big picture focus. They are able to see beyond the immediate and look at things in a bigger, broader, and long-term way.

My personal favorite example of one such person who I think of as a great example of a visionary thinker is Taylor Swift. Some might think of her as unconventional or cliché, but look at what she's done. It's incredible. She took back her master resell rights, rerecorded her albums so that she would get all of her IP back, and she was able to see what that was going to do for her future in the business. From there, she created a tour where she took her audiences on a journey through all of her past albums through the different eras, which created incredible brand loyalty. She did this in a way that everybody was excited to buy tickets and be part of the experience. She made it a global tour, and stretched it out for many, many months. She tapped into what her people were wanting and where she was seeing this brand loyalty pop up. In the process, she created a new album and added it to her current tour, which was already sold out. That's unbelievable visionary thinking. Her brand is solid gold. Her followers are so loyal that they know the story of her, but also all of her albums and all of her songs. She plays back to things that she said in the past so that people have an even stronger connection. Doing this creates all kinds of verticals with her merchandise and allows for different types of ways to buy her music. For example, she'll record an acoustic version of all the music she performed on one of her tours giving her a new source of revenue and a new way of hearing her music for her loyal fans. They are buying the same music but with a completely different way of listening to it.

This woman's vision is incredible. She looks into the future, sees what people are going to want, and it's based all on brand loyalty. She has the ability to connect with a huge global audience in such a way they don't even have to meet her in person to know everything about her, what she's doing and where she's going to the point they even track her plane. For crying out loud, it is unbelievable. So, yes, definitely a visionary thinker. She has top-notch business savvy and takes really bold moves to get to the next level. With that, she affects the lives of everyone that is part of her journey. She is able to empower her team, her dancers, her leaders, her marketing people, and gets everybody on board with her vision.

Vision has always been my strength. I can see it crystal clear, and I love painting the picture of what that dream looks like and how it will positively affect everyone. Follow through is not my strength, but I know this and my team knows this, so we need people on the team who are dreamers and doers and those who inspire accountability.

2. Emotional Intelligence:

Empathy: Understand and address the emotions, motivations, and concerns of team members. A good leader can put themselves in the place of the people they lead, and in fact, have most of the time literally been in their position in the past. That's not to say all leaders must rise from the ranks, but it means that the leader understands the roles of the people who are in their charge. They know what it takes to do those jobs or have those positions, and can therefore understand their issues and needs at a deep level.

Self-Awareness: Recognize your own strengths and weaknesses and how they impact others. This is very important. If you don't know your strengths as a leader, you need to do some self-discovery and learn what you are best at, what you can bring to your leadership, your strongest skills, and even more importantly, your weak spots. It's okay to be weak in some areas. It's not okay to pretend you're perfect and have no weaknesses. Owning who you are and being authentic in that knowledge will take you a long way as a leader.

3. Courage and Vulnerability:

Taking Risks: Show a willingness to step into the unknown and make bold decisions, even in the face of uncertainty. This is not easy. Can you imagine, young Dorothy, having landed in a strange and sometimes frightening land, crushing one wicked witch only to deal with an even worse one, now having to step into the complete unknown? She did it, though, one step at a time. Talk about risks! But as they say, no risk, no reward. Sometimes your bold decision will end in a flop, even a disaster, but that can't be a reason to play it safe.

During the pandemic, my heart was broken for my team. For the first time, I couldn't see the vision. I didn't know what was going to happen next. On that fateful Friday the 13th of March, I broke down in front of my team and I said, "I don't know WHAT is going to happen next or HOW we are going to make it work, but I promise you I will do everything in my power to keep you employed full-time for as long as I can, so you can keep your jobs."

Admitting Mistakes: Own up to failures and view them as opportunities for growth and learning. There are no failures, only different ways to move forward. Leaders who pretend they never make mistakes are soon seen as a fake. We are humans. We will screw up, and I mean often. I certainly have, and likely I will again. The trick is to say, "That's on me. I got that wrong and I'm sorry." Not that hard, right?

4. Adaptability and Resilience:

Flexibility: Be open to change and new ideas, and adapt strategies as needed. If you take the stance that you are always right or that the only way to do things is the way they have always been done, you may struggle as a leader. A good leader is open-minded and willing to listen and learn. If this concept feels uncomfortable, remember we learn a lot more when we are uncomfortable than when we're at ease. Things change in every field. Growth comes when we are adaptable, not rigid in our thinking or methodologies.

Persistence: Stay focused and committed to your goals, even when faced with challenges and setbacks. Great leaders don't quit when the going gets tough. There will always be difficult times and times when things go wrong. The trick is to stay calm and keep moving toward the goals you've set. This could take you back to the idea of flexibility. Challenges are just learning experiences, and being able to navigate them and still remain committed to the end result is one sign of great leadership.

5. Relationship Building:

Trust and Respect: Building and maintaining trust through consistent actions and respect for others is key to leadership. People will follow leaders who they respect and trust far beyond expectations. But remember, trust and respect are two-way streets. To gain them, you have to give them. Being in charge, being the leader, doesn't automatically mean you will have the respect of the people you lead. This has to be earned. Be trustworthy and respectful of others. Great leaders know the importance of this.

Collaboration: Foster a collaborative environment where everyone feels valued and heard. You don't know everything, and that's a good thing. This goes back to what I said about listening. You may not adapt every idea suggested by staff or employees, but letting them know they can come to you with their ideas, problems, and suggestions will make them know you care about their needs, and it isn't just your way or no way. You will be surprised at what can be gained by collaborating rather than dictating.

6. Ethical Standards:

Integrity: Acting with honesty and integrity in all dealings is the most important part of being a leader. Leading from a place of honor and respect for the work and the people you work with is the sign of great leadership. People will see through a leader who isn't truthful or who has an agenda that's not in alignment with the mission and purpose of the organization. You can't fake integrity!

Accountability: Hold oneself and others accountable for their actions. Leadership is hard. You WILL mess up, I promise. That's no big deal. What is a big deal is not owning up to your mistakes. And you can't ask anyone else to be accountable for their mistakes, if you are not willing to be accountable for yours. Would you follow a leader who can never say, "I was wrong," or, "I made a mistake and I'm sorry about that." ? Not likely, and not many people would.

Accountability used to be right up there with good operator for me. I could not hold anyone accountable because I was the girl of a million chances. My trauma shone through in my addiction to people pleasing. However, necessity breeds abundance, and during the great resignation, I had no choice but to come up with a better way to hold my team accountable, to raise quality, and to reward the A team! Due to the fact that I myself am not good at accountability, I had to come up with a system and to get buy in from my team to make sure we stuck to it. That is when I created our *Practically Perfect Performance Scorecard System* for our team to measure performance and KPI's. This was a game changer for our company, and now hundreds of other childcare owners use my system for success in their businesses. I did lose employees and even friends over this, but this system of accountability was what was needed to raise the quality of my business.

IS LEADERSHIP FOR YOU?

Answer these questions as honestly as you can.

1. Do You Have a Clear Vision?

Can you see where you want to lead your team or organization in the next five to ten years?

_____

_____

_____

2. Are You Empathetic and Emotionally Intelligent?

Do you genuinely care about the well-being and development of those you lead?

_____

_____

_____

3. Can You Handle Uncertainty and Risk?**

Are you comfortable making decisions without all the answers and taking responsibility for the outcomes?

_____

_____

_____

4. Are You Adaptable?

Can you pivot and adjust your strategies when circumstances change?

_____

_____

_____

5. Do You Build Strong Relationships?

Are you skilled at building trust and fostering collaboration among diverse groups of people?

_____

_____

_____

6. Do You Uphold High Ethical Standards?

Do you consistently act with integrity and hold yourself accountable?

_____

_____

_____

Reflect on Your Experiences

- ☐ **Past Leadership Roles:** Reflect on any previous leadership roles or experiences. What did you enjoy? What were the challenges? How did you handle them?

- ☐ **Feedback from Others:** Seek feedback from colleagues, mentors, or team members about your leadership style and effectiveness.

- ☐ **Personal Passion:** Do you feel passionate about leading and making a difference in your organization or community?

So, is leadership for you? Does everyone need to be or should be a leader? Let's talk more about it in the next chapter.

CHAPTER 5

(G) GROUNDED IN RUBY SLIPPERS

I need reminders to stay grounded. I often feel like I'm all over the place. I have a lot of balls in the air, multiple schools, lots of employees, and many, many, students who are my responsibility. I think of the Ruby Slippers as a visual reminder to look down and stay grounded. But they are pretty, fun, and playful. Part of being grounded is just that… remembering to be playful and have fun.

"There's no place like home."

This iconic line from *The Wonderful Wizard of Oz* encapsulates the idea that, despite life's complexities, grounding oneself in the familiar and embracing a sense of playfulness can provide comfort and stability. Recently, my family and I moved into a new home, embarking on a journey of purging, downsizing, and simplifying our lives. This process has ushered in a refreshing domestic era for me—a time to reconnect with my roots and find joy in creating a more intentional and balanced space.

While this shift has brought me back to the essence of home and family, it has also deepened my appreciation for my career and business life. This duality reminds me that being grounded doesn't mean choosing one side of myself over the other; instead, it's about embracing both the playful, nurturing aspects of home and the ambitious, driven side of my leadership journey. Together, these pieces create a foundation where I can thrive both personally and professionally.

Shoes have always been more than just a practical necessity for me—they are a source of joy, confidence, and self-expression. I've always loved shoes, from classic heels to playful sneakers, each pair telling a story about who I am and how I'm feeling on any given day. Shoes are the finishing touch of an outfit, the detail that pulls everything together and transforms the ordinary into something extraordinary. There's something magical about slipping into the perfect pair—they have the power to make you stand taller, walk bolder, and face the world with just a little more confidence.

But for me, shoes are more than just an accessory; they're a metaphor for life and leadership. Like a great pair of shoes, being grounded in who you are is essential to navigating the world with purpose and confidence. This is where the idea of ruby slippers comes in—they're my playful reminder to stay grounded and centered amidst the chaos of running multiple schools, managing teams, and balancing life's many demands.

Just like Dorothy's ruby slippers guided her home, my love for shoes reminds me that being grounded doesn't mean being stuck—it's about standing firm while embracing creativity, fun, and the confidence to take the next step. Shoes have this way of carrying us forward while also keeping us rooted in the moment, and that's the kind of energy I aim to bring to both my personal life and my leadership journey. Whether I'm in heels commanding a room, sneakers chasing after a child, or barefoot finding my center, I know that staying grounded and embracing the magic of life's small details is what keeps me balanced and thriving.

Remembering to make things beautiful but also functional. Those pretty ruby slippers held up all the way along the *Yellow Brick Road*, and they kept the witch at bay. In the end, all it took to get home was to click their heels three times. Talk about functional. Remembering them and having fun even while working helps me have balance. I think a good leader learns to balance being grounded and still able to enjoy their life and allow themselves and the people they lead to tackle work with joy and playfulness.

Growing up, life wasn't very easy for me, but I didn't let that hold me back, and to be honest, I didn't really notice the challenges. As an adult, I often wondered why some people carry the weight of their childhood into adulthood in a crippling way, while others use their experiences as tools and lessons. What differentiates these two paths?

Watching Allie struggle with ADHD was one of the most heart-wrenching experiences of my life. She had trouble accomplishing tasks, fitting in socially, and keeping up with her schoolwork. As a mother, I watched her pain, helplessly witnessing her fall into attention-seeking behaviors and, ultimately, turning to drugs and alcohol as an escape. The parallels to my own father's addiction terrified me. The fear that Allie would suffer the same fate haunted me daily. Not knowing how to help her, I buried myself in work, throwing all my energy into searching for solutions—for her and for the next generation of children like her.

In that search, I discovered research from *Harvard's Center on the Developing Child*, and it completely shifted my perspective—not just as a mother, but as a leader. The studies on resilience were eye-opening. According to Harvard's findings, resilience is not something we are born with but something that can be developed. One of the most critical factors in building resilience in children is the presence of a stable, supportive adult in their lives. They need a "champion," someone who believes in them unconditionally and helps guide them through adversity.

This idea resonated with me deeply. Allie had been struggling for so long, and while I thought I was doing everything I could as her mother, I realized I had not always been the champion she needed. I had been present physically, but emotionally, I had often been distracted by work and the demands of life. The Harvard research made it clear that children—especially those facing adversity like Allie with her ADHD—need more than just a parent. They need someone who will stand by them, help them build resilience, and give them the tools to thrive, despite the challenges.

The ACES Study

Then, I came across the Adverse Childhood Experiences (ACES) study, which made me even more aware of how critical it is to have that support in place. The ACES study is one of the most comprehensive investigations into the long-term impact of childhood trauma, and its findings are staggering. The study found that children who experience a high number of adverse childhood experiences—such as trauma, neglect, or growing up with a parent who struggles with addiction—are more likely to face significant physical and mental health challenges later in life. This includes a higher risk of substance abuse, depression, anxiety, and even chronic illnesses like heart disease and diabetes.

What struck me about the ACES study was the clear connection between childhood adversity and long-term outcomes, but even more important was the evidence showing these negative outcomes are not inevitable. The research revealed that a stable, supportive relationship with a caring adult could mitigate many of the harmful effects of adverse experiences. That relationship—whether it's with a parent, teacher, or mentor—provides a sense of safety and connection, which is critical for children as they develop emotional resilience.

Rita Pierson, a well-known educator, once said, "Every child deserves a champion—an adult who will never give up on them, who understands the power of connection and insists that they become the best that they can possibly be." That's exactly what I realized I needed to be for Allie. It wasn't too late for her, and I knew that if I could show up for her in a more consistent, supportive way, she could start to rebuild her resilience. I could be her champion, just as I wanted to be for every child in the programs I've created through my work.

As I reflected on this, I realized the same principles applied to my team. Just like children, adults also face their own forms of adversity—whether it's personal struggles, workplace stress, or feelings of inadequacy. We may not call them "champions" in the adult world, but as a leader, I see now that my role is to be that supportive figure for my team. The lessons I learned from Harvard's research and the ACES study aren't just relevant for children—they apply to leadership, too.

Just like Allie needed someone to help her build resilience, my team needs someone who can guide them through challenges, help them recognize their strengths, and provide the emotional support they need to thrive. Too often, we think of leadership in terms of goals, performance metrics, and outcomes. But what I've come to understand is that leadership is about connection. It's about being grounded, present, and emotionally attuned to the needs of those around us.

The research shows that resilience is built through relationships, and that's exactly how I approach my role as a leader now. I'm not just the person who sets the vision or drives the strategy—I'm also the person who helps my team members navigate their own struggles, whether they're personal or professional. Just as Harvard's research emphasized the importance of a stable, supportive relationship for children, I've realized creating a strong, trusting relationship with my team members is essential for their growth and success.

This means showing up consistently, being emotionally available, and creating a work environment where people feel safe to be vulnerable. I can't always fix every problem they face, but I can be there to support them, help them build resilience, and remind them they have the strength to overcome whatever challenges come their way.

Grounding myself as a leader means recognizing that vulnerability is not a weakness—it's a strength. It's about admitting when I don't have all the answers and being open about my own struggles, just like I had to confront my fears with Allie. By doing this, I can create a culture where my team feels comfortable coming to me with their challenges, knowing that I will support them and help them find solutions.

The ACES study also taught me the importance of early intervention. Whether it's with children or with my team, it's crucial to address problems before they escalate. If I can be proactive in offering support, providing resources, and fostering resilience, I can help prevent burnout, disengagement, and other negative outcomes. Just like with Allie, if I catch the signs early and step in as a supportive leader, I can make a significant difference.

In the end, being a champion for my team is about much more than being a boss or a manager. It's about building deep, trusting relationships that help people thrive—not just in their work but in their lives. Just as Allie needed me to show up for her in a deeper way, my team needs me to be present, grounded, and fully invested in their well-being. If I can do that, I know we'll not only overcome adversity but also create something truly remarkable together.

I realized I had been fortunate to have multiple champions in my life: my grandparents, brother, mother, father, and even my husband, who came into my life when I was just 13. Like Dorothy in *The Wizard of Oz*, I found my champions along the *Yellow Brick Road*. I knew I had to be that champion for Allie. I'm happy to say that today, Allie is one of my best friends, living a clean, successful life, and about to become a mother.

This experience taught me a great deal about leadership and the importance of being grounded. When I named this chapter, I initially thought of "Ruby Slippers," because they are beautiful and functional, reflecting my mantra that everything should be both. But being grounded goes much deeper. It's about knowing who you are, the direction you're heading, and having at least one champion to guide you on your path.

Denzel Washington once said, "Show me a successful individual and I'll show you someone who had real positive influences in his or her life. I don't care what you do for a living—if you do it well, I'm sure there was someone cheering you on or showing the way. A mentor."

Recently, a mentor I am working with asked me how I stay grounded. No one had ever asked me that before. I had to think about that, but one thing I knew is that I have had people in my life who inspired me and helped me stay grounded. One such person is Julie Roy. Julie is not only an inspiration; she is a treasured friend.

Julie is a successful, serial entrepreneur with two large multinational businesses. She was the Founder, Owner/Operator of Montessori Preschools from 2001-2021, both in the USA and Canada. She is the leader of a group I'm excited to be part of, "WEALTHMASTERS." It's a business mastermind coaching program for business owners like myself. She helps us with our goals to scale, exit, and/or build legacy wealth. Her husband Beau is a retired psychologist, they are parents to four beautiful kiddos, and they work together as real estate investors, perfecting long-term legacy and wealth for them and for the future of their children

Julie is very similar to me in many ways. We are both ADHD, moms of four, and full of ambition for not only ourselves but for our families and the people in our lives who count on us. She helps me ground myself, constantly reminding me to focus on what I need, and to put my energy into what really matters. I think it's ironic someone with ADHD is the one person who best shows me how to focus. Julie has hyperfocus. She will say, "You need to focus on this thing. This other thing isn't gonna give you the ROI you're going for. If it's not one of your strengths, don't focus on it." She knows my end game. She helps me keep on that path, eye on the prize. She is grounded with her family as I strive to be as well. She's inspiring as a wife and mother and is uber protective of her family's growth, creating their legacy wealth as well as their knowledge of cultures of the world, giving them unbelievable life experiences. Her family comes above all else. She's made me a much better leader and mom, and I have grown exponentially around the parameters of my family and my work from our friendship and her mentorship.

One of my first mentors in business was Alix Hall. I was in awe of her beauty, confidence, intelligence, and success. Alix owns six schools in Sacramento, which she started when she was just 19. She became a leader in her community and in the early childhood education field. When I met her, I owned two schools but felt lost and was faking it every step of the way. Alix taught me how to run a multisite organization, dream bigger, and remain focused on the big picture. We became best friends, and she was like a sister to me. I wouldn't be where I am today without her guidance and support.

Alix introduced me to the concept of WWAD—What Would Alix Do? This simple question transformed into a guiding principle for our organization, shaping our standard operating procedures. It evolved into WWRD—What Would Rachel Do?—and became the foundation for our operations manual. I taught my leaders to create SOPs by asking themselves this same question. A tip for creating effective SOPs is to involve your team in the process. Encourage them to document their tasks step-by-step and review these procedures regularly to ensure they are up-to-date and efficient. This collaborative approach not only creates comprehensive SOPs but also empowers your team to take ownership of their roles.

Having strong role models, mentors, and powerful friendships with people you aspire to be like, is a big component of getting and staying grounded. Seek those people and create those relationships. It's immeasurable.

As I have made clear, I truly believe that a critical aspect of leadership is play. As a recovering workaholic, I know the value of hard work, but I've also experienced burnout, marital issues, health problems, and business mistakes due to a lack of play. Mr. Rogers once said, "Play is often talked about as if it were a relief from serious learning. But for children, play is serious learning. Play is really the work of childhood."

Research shows that play is essential not only for children but also for leaders. It enhances creativity, reduces stress, and improves overall well-being. Leaders who incorporate play into their routines are more innovative and resilient, and they are able to stay grounded in what matters.

Here are some tips to integrate play into your leadership practice:

- **Brain Breaks:** Short, frequent breaks can boost productivity and creativity.

- **Laughter:** Find humor in everyday situations.

- **Noticing Triggers:** Be aware of stressors and address them promptly.

- **Managing Energy:** Prioritize tasks based on your energy levels.

- **Not Taking Everything Seriously:** Learn to let go and enjoy the moment.

- **Mini Breaks:** Incorporate brief moments of relaxation throughout the day.

- **Prioritizing:** Focus on what truly matters.

- **Main Event:** Plan activities that bring joy and relaxation.

The ruby slippers symbolize staying grounded and having the right path, with champions guiding you. The beauty of the slippers represents the importance of play. To remain grounded as a leader, you need both mentorship and play.

ACTION ITEMS

☐ How do I stay grounded? How to protect my ability to do so?

☐ Reflection: I take the time to reflect on the things I am grateful for. Gratitude is a key to grounding you in the good in your life and expelling the negativity that sends you off the rails.

I protect my summer with my life. I don't travel or speak during summer months, though I am asked often to do so. Mondays and Fridays in summer are protected. I load up my schedule Tuesdays through Thursdays, leaving the long weekend for my family and our summer activities. I protect our fun.

I consider the seasons of each year. During football season, I know that a good part of my time is in watching my boys play this sport they love.

I am more grounded when I am barefoot in sunshine and on or near the water. That's easy in the summer in my home state of Montana but impossible in the winter. So, I travel in winter to get into the sun and out of the harsh Montana winters. I choose speaking engagements, seminars, and conferences, and working with clients in warmer climates as often as possible during the winter.

I use breathing techniques and meditation to calm my overactive mind and my ADHD.

While I am an extrovert at heart and truly love people, I really need my alone time. I have to have it, or I will lose my creativity and joy.

When worries and concerns send me into a spin, I use my technique of considering the worst thing that could happen and explore what I would do if that came to pass. Quieting my mind and assuaging my fears is a form of self-soothing and keeps me grounded and motivated, too.

CHAPTER 6:

IMPOSTER SYNDROME

My parents used the money we needed for food or gas to send us to a private school, hoping to set us up for success. Unfortunately, the drawback was that the financial disparity between me and the rest of the school just made my struggle worse. The feeling I would never be good enough solidified itself in my mind. I did my best to become a social chameleon to fight off these feelings, distracting others from my own low self-esteem by finessing my social skills and mastering my role playing to forge an idealistic persona. But I knew I couldn't tolerate this forever. I needed to escape for real.

Being a Chameleon:

I met my husband when we were in high school. We went to the same school, but we did not have the same family life. He was from a middle class family with a good income and a nice home. He wanted to come to my house, but I was embarrassed for him to see where I lived. We were too young to drive, so my mom drove us places and the day he was supposed to come to the house, she dropped me off first and drove him around the block a couple times to let me have time to clean up. I grabbed a couple of giant trash bags and tossed everything in them, putting it all in the laundry room. I wanted things to be at least presentable the first time he came over.

My mom's car was repossessed so often that we were in the habit of looking out the window to see if it was there every morning before we went anywhere. The car broke down a lot. One time, it did so in the school parking lot when she came to pick me up. Mom flagged down a couple students, teen boys, to ask them to push the car. It was a standard shift and the parking lot was flat so, they had to get it really moving for her to pop it into gear and get it going. I was horrified. Today, I would likely laugh it off, but not as a sensitive teen.

Our high school was mission-minded. We went to chapel weekly and gave our offerings. Once a month, the offering went to a poor family. Each month, I was terrified that they would call my family's name. I would hold my breath every time they said the name of the family receiving the blessing and let go of my breath when it wasn't us.

The school did not require us to wear uniforms. The rich kids all wore designer clothes and shoes, had fancy purses, and the best sneakers for athletics. Our stuff came from thrift stores. My brother had it worse than I did. He often had to wear my hand-me-downs. He even wore pink shoes and peach slacks one year.

As much as I have moved away from all that and I know that I am a success, I am, in a way, embarrassed to say that now I have all kinds of designer stuff. The house I grew up in was the size of my living room now. All my friends in high school had giant, amazing homes, not unlike the houses I own now. It was a private school and the families chose to go there. Kids were driven in from all over the San Diego area. Trust me, these were high-end people and we were very poor. I wanted what they had for my future life and had a *I am never gonna be enough* syndrome. Today, it is still hard to say I am proud of myself and look back to see all I have accomplished. I still feel like it's not enough, or it's never going to be enough.

So, how does a leader work through that? How do we lead even when we suffer from Imposter Syndrome?

My answer: The best way to get over imposter syndrome is to serve others.

Imposter syndrome is a cycle. It repeats itself, and you have to stop and recognize the triggers and what your why is. The real cure is serving others. It's not about your mission and vision. It doesn't matter if you think you are not enough. It's not about you. It's about who you will serve and why, and what you are serving others. I have taken very impactful training on imposter syndrome and have learned a lot about what makes big successful companies thrive.

It's not thinking about the bottom line or the end game. It's about who we are serving. I love helping people. I have 10 locations. We serve over 1,000 children. How many family and community members are being served by what we do? Because of my business, many women have jobs and a chance to level up. They get to serve others and feel good about who they are and what they do. We serve children and affect their lives. Big businesses affect far more than their employees, clients, and customers. Their efforts create a domino effect.

I've created a metric for how to move away from imposter syndrome, so that you can move toward serving others and away from your own insecurities.

Imposter syndrome starts when….

- You begin or are assigned a new project or task.

- You procrastinate or over-prepare for the work.

- You complete the project and have a brief moment of relief.

- You rationalize that success – I got lucky this time.

- Next there is the spike of self-doubt—I am a fraud—or you overwork to prove yourself.

Instead of all that, think…

- Who is this for, and how can I serve that person or group? It's not about your accomplishment but the people you serve.

- Realize the impact this project will make.

- Know the project is serving others by your work and take the focus off YOU! Stop being self-absorbed. What good will come of it and what will be the far reaching effects of your accomplishment?

As a leader, you will dance a fine line of propelling yourself forward and serving others. It's easy to slip into a selfish nature. *These are my goals. I have to do all this.* This happens especially with highly driven people. If you run a fairly big company like I do, or bigger, it's your team that will get you there.

I know it's my vision, but my team drives the train. It's not about the money or having enough. It's about the team and blessing people, impacting people, helping more leaders grow, and more women succeed. Why would I stop doing that?

Fighting imposter syndrome is well worth it, and I do it every day.

"If you weren't ready, you simply wouldn't have the opportunity!" That is it!! It is actually that simple. God gives us opportunities when you are ready for them and you cannot stress. Surrender what you cannot control. You have the opportunity to be great, do your very best and put it in the universe. Imposter syndrome can be your biggest storm to overcome.

Speaking of storms….

The Most Well-Known Imposter - The Wizard

The Wizard is the ultimate example of imposter syndrome. In reality, he was a little man afraid of people finding out he was not big enough or good enough to lead them, so he created this farce. There is a line in the movie where Dorothy confronts him once she knows the truth.

"You are a very bad man!" she says.

"Oh, no my dear, I am very good man. I'm just a very bad wizard."

And he was actually a good man. In the end, he uses his goodness and his intelligence to give all of them what they needed. Moreover, he saw in them the skills, traits, and abilities he didn't have. He got them to use their talents to accomplish the task of destroying the witch.

Sometimes, you can't do it all yourself, and it's a huge mistake to try. It creates pressure that will make you fail. Give tasks to the people who can accomplish those tasks. The Wizard wanted the people of the Emerald City to be safe from the Wicked Witch. So he sent them off on a difficult task, but he saw in them that they could accomplish this with their heart, brains, courage, and Dorothy's determination.

Remember that it's not about you, it's about the big picture. It's about the team. It's good to utilize the skills of the team to accomplish tasks. Imposter syndrome might tell you otherwise, that it's all on you, but if you allow the team to be involved, it helps them get over their fears and imposter syndrome and the job gets done!

Systems and tools help fight Imposter Syndrome

My daughter, Abbie, leads our summer camps and this year is one of our biggest camps ever with 120 kids and a lot of staff. I know this can become overwhelming. A lot of what we do in my business is stressful, and there is a ton of responsibility working with kids and families.

As a leader, it's my job to help my staff get over the overwhelm, and I realize that a lot of it comes down to their belief in their abilities to do the tasks they're given. It means fighting the urge to sink into imposter syndrome. It starts with me. I have to have systems in place to fight my own imposter syndrome, and I don't want my children to fall into their own version of this.

My kids don't tell people at work that they're my kids. We want them to earn their own way at work and in life and not use the privilege of their name or position. They all work for us in one way or the other. Our oldest daughter runs our summer camps, our oldest son is in maintenance, our youngest son helps with camps, and our youngest daughter helps teach the little kids. By not making them feel like they have their jobs just because of some form of nepotism can help manage their self-esteem or self-doubt issues.

We expect them to do the work like everyone else in the company and that way they know they are valuable and accomplished in their own right.

Tools Help

I have some tools that help my directors and teachers to create a better system for themselves to quell the overwhelm and self-doubts, I use these systems myself.

It starts with creating good habits to help you manage the energy you're putting into the work. When you adopt a servant leadership mentality, you change the energy to one that focuses on the outcome of the tasks you have to accomplish. There is a Swahili saying *sawubona*, which means, *I see you, I hear you*. You are here to value and serve people.

If I have leaders struggling with imposter syndrome, I make them see that they can help someone else manage their imposter syndrome, and by teaching it, they can manage their own fears and self-doubts. It will always be there, make no mistake. I suffer this often, but I've learned to manage and recognize it and to flip it. It won't happen until you use what you learn to teach and serve others. My directors help my teachers, and my teachers help their students, which can change the world. It's a trickle-down effect.

Systems are everything—seeing when this is happening or someone is having anxiety. Having tools that must be used daily, creates a system to help my staff and I manage the issues that can slow us down or stop us in our tracks.

Here are some things we do with our staff:

The Gratitude Walk

Often, when a director is about to walk into their building, they are bombarded with issues, problems, fires, and emergencies. They might have started their day in a great mood, with positivity. If they get overwhelmed and overrun with issues, it can change their energy and set them on the wrong path. They end the day feeling defeated and like nothing was accomplished. This feeds their self-doubts.

We don't allow that to happen. The staff knows the director is to do their gratitude walk before starting the day and nothing is to be brought to their attention to interrupt them before that happens. It starts with them walking the four corners of the property, walking the whole way around the outside of the building. Then, they choose one classroom to walk the four walls corner to corner. This takes about 15 minutes. While walking, they focus on something they are grateful for that day.

The teachers do their gratitude walk around the four corners of their classroom before starting their day as well. They all do this every day. It is part of their scorecard. "Did you do your Gratitude Walk each day?" is a question they must answer.

The Daily 5

I have extreme ADHD, and I have a bad tendency to procrastinate. Add to that I am great at finding the hardest way to get to things going over the meadow, through the woods, and over the mountain to get to the result. I also admit I have a hard time separating work and home. Does that track with you at all?

What I do for myself, and now have my staff doing as well, is what I call The Daily Five. We keep a journal in the car and before we leave home, we write five things in the journal we need to address or is a frustration from home. This can be something we need to do later, a thing that is upsetting us, or some drama that doesn't need to be dealt with while we're at work. We do the same thing when leaving work, leaving work issues in the car written in the journal to deal with when we get back to work the next day. It helps keep work stuff at work and home stuff at home. This is a great way to reduce stress and overwhelm. Sometimes, it is a huge help to just stop, take a deep breath before dumping it all onto paper, and move on.

Brain Dump

Brain dumping can fight the urge to slip into imposter syndrome. As a leader, you don't want to fail other people, especially those that count on you. We can feel that you're being judged but that's you thinking you're not good enough. It's not coming from anyone else.

We use a technique I call the Brain Dump. I ask my staff to do this daily as well as part of their responsibilities. The idea is to list the top five priorities they want to complete for the day. If they get stuck and can't accomplish something by the end of the day, they have to consider how to change that. Do they need help? Are there resources they need to utilize? They must ask themselves, *why did I not complete this*? Then, they put that task on the list for the next day and find a way to tackle it. I ask them to identify the most important thing on their daily list, the main event, and focus their energy on that task. If they focus on what they can do, the energy they put out will drive them to accomplish that task.

When we focus on what we can't do, those tasks will never get done. "I'm not good enough?" "Why did she pick me?" "I will let her down." These kinds of thoughts will seep in, but I encourage my staff members to focus on the things they are going to do. That way, the flow of energy will come to that task, and they will accomplish it usually with ease. Negative beliefs about a task will stop the flow of energy to that task.

Work Backwards to Reach the Goal

When you or someone under your leadership has a big thing to accomplish, the thing to do is to work backwards. What do I need to accomplish? Start there and consider the tasks to get to the end result from the last one to the first. When you get overwhelmed and think this can't be done, think about the worst thing that can happen. If it did happen, what would you do? Consider the outcome and the best path to deal with it and come out the best way possible.

It's my responsibility to see that the leaders in my staff have the tools to manage their imposter syndrome. I have asked several of my leaders what their biggest fear is being a director or leader in one of our schools. The most common answer I got was, "I don't want to let you down." That's terrible! I never want anyone to feel that way, and it's not a thing. It's not gonna happen.

I get the thought process they go through. "She's entrusted me with this great responsibility!" "I don't see what she sees in me." It's my job as a leader to empower them to do their jobs. I have the faith they can do what's required of them, but it is up to them to find the tools to get there and use the ones we've established. I truly believe the adage that God only gives you what you can handle. If there is a mountain you are given to climb, you are fully capable of climbing it or it wouldn't have been given to you. It's your job to plan how you will execute the climb, what training you have to do, and what supplies you will need—clothing, boots, food, and water. I give my staff responsibilities, but I also give them the room to find the road to handle those responsibilities. When they get lost, I will redirect them to find the tools and use them; breathing, doing the daily five, the brain dump, and the gratitude walk.

ACTION ITEMS

1. Conduct a Gratitude Walk

☐ Before starting your day, take a 5-15 minute walk around your workspace.

☐ Focus on the four corners of the property and one classroom or office.

☐ During your walk, think about one thing you are grateful for today.

Reflection:

☐ What are you grateful for today?

☐ How did the gratitude walk affect your mindset as you began your day?

2. Perform a Daily Brain Dump

☐ Keep a journal in your car or workspace.

☐ Each day, write down five things that are on your mind, whether work-related or personal.

Reflection:

- ☐ What are the five things on your mind today?
- ☐ How does writing them down help you focus on the present tasks?

3. Implement The Daily 5

- ☐ At the start of each day, list the top five priorities you need to accomplish.
- ☐ Identify the most important task (the "main event") and focus your energy on it.

Reflection:

- ☐ What are your top five priorities for today?
- ☐ What is your "main event" task, and why is it the most important?

4. Use the Work Backwards Technique

- ☐ Identify a significant goal you need to accomplish.
- ☐ Work backwards from the goal, listing the steps needed to achieve it from the end to the beginning.

Reflection:

- ☐ What is your significant goal?
- ☐ What are the steps required to achieve this goal, starting from the end?

5. Develop and Use Support Systems

☐ Identify tools and systems that help you manage imposter syndrome (e.g., gratitude walks, brain dumps, The Daily 5).

☐ Implement these tools consistently and encourage your team to use them as well.

Reflection:

☐ What tools and systems are you using to manage imposter syndrome?

☐ How do these tools help you and your team stay focused and productive?

CHAPTER 7

(I) INFLUENCE-
CREATING A MAGNETIC
COLLABORATIVE CULTURE

*"Entrusted to us so that we might
form stability out of chaos"*
- Morgan Freeman (Wanted – The movie)

Who are your Scarecrow, Tin Man, and Cowardly Lion?

W hat we all crave in the world of leadership is influence. Influence is everything. It is the invisible force that pulls people together, drives passion, and ignites commitment to a shared vision. True leadership is about using that influence to create a culture where people not only want to follow you but are excited to bring others along on the crazy journey. At Discovery Kidzone, influence goes beyond titles and authority. In fact, I really despise "authority." Influence is about creating a magnetic, collaborative culture where people feel a deep connection to the mission, the values, and each other. In essence, it is MAGIC.

When I promote a director, they get a necklace with a tribe symbol on it. My husband is Native American, and I want my directors to know that they are part of the tribe. I have that same symbol tattooed on my leg. Most of my directors have gotten the same tattoo, even our new directors. I do NOT MAKE them to do this, just for the record. They are simply enthusiastic about our "tribe," our mission, and our values. They love the work and the way we operate our schools.

My leadership team is strong, tight, and amazing. But not everyone is a good fit and sometimes when someone quits in any kind of toxic way, rumors spread that we are some kind of cult. "When you work for them, you better get it that you'll become part of their cult." Um… no! We do have strong influence with our staff, and our team is happy and loves what we do. If this makes people feel like we are a cult or we give off the aura that we are a cult, that's on them!

True leadership is about influence. As a leader, you will influence others to want to work with you, to buy into your vision, and your company culture. Influence is how you expand and grow your vision and big picture. Influence shows your passion and allows you to pass that passion onto the leaders of your staff. Then, they get to do the same passing of that passion down to others.

Childcare is total chaos. For us, to be able to form stability, we have to have leaders in the organization who are entrusted with the vision, the big picture, where we are going, so we are all headed in the right direction

Nothing is autonomous. We are all a piece of the puzzle, and the mission is bigger than ourselves.

John Maxwell famously said, "Leadership is influence, nothing more, nothing less."

This notion shifts the focus from the position one holds to the impact they have on the people around them. As a leader, your goal is to inspire others to follow, not because they have to, but because they want to. Peer influence plays a significant role in this dynamic.

Every leader has a "sphere of influence"—a network of peers, direct reports, and even superiors, who are impacted by their actions and decisions. This concept is central to effective leadership, as your ability to drive change depends on how well you can influence those within your sphere.

To expand your sphere of influence, you must focus on three key areas:

- Credibility

- Communication

- Connection

1. **Credibility:** This is the foundation of influence. If people don't trust you, your ability to influence them will be severely diminished. Leaders build credibility by consistently delivering on promises, demonstrating expertise, and showing empathy. Empathy can be hard for some people, especially if you are like me and your "give a shit broke," so, you will have to work harder to foster empathy. Credibility also comes from

vulnerability—showing that you are human and that you, too, face challenges. This authenticity fosters deeper connections and more meaningful influence.

2. **Communication:** Clear, consistent, and compelling communication is critical for influencing others. Those are the 5 C's to remember. Leaders who communicate their vision with clarity are more likely to inspire others to follow. But communication is not just about talking; it's also about listening. Effective leaders listen to the needs, concerns, and aspirations of their team. When people feel seen, heard, and valued, they are more likely to be influenced by you.

3. **Connection:** Building authentic relationships is at the heart of peer influence. People are more likely to be influenced by those they feel connected to on a personal level. Leaders who invest in understanding their peers' values, motivations, and concerns create stronger bonds that lead to greater influence. Peer relationships are not hierarchical; they are horizontal. By treating your peers as equals and collaborators, you strengthen your ability to influence them.

Creating Early Adopters: In any organizational change, there are early adopters—those who are quick to embrace new ideas and behaviors. These individuals can serve as powerful influencers within their peer groups, and something I had to learn the hard way when working through acquisitions. Leaders should identify and cultivate relationships with early adopters, empowering them to spread influence throughout the organization.

Social Proof and Bandwagon Effect: People are more likely to follow the crowd. They won't follow you, until it is popular. When peers within a group begin to shift their behavior, others are inclined to follow to avoid being left behind. As a leader, strategically using social proof can create a tipping point where new norms and behaviors become the standard across the organization.

The Role of Reciprocity and Liking: According to Robert Cialdini's work on influence, two powerful psychological principles—reciprocity and liking—are key drivers in influencing others. In the context of peer influence, these principles can be leveraged to build stronger relationships and inspire action.

Reciprocity: People tend to feel obligated to return favors or kindnesses. Leaders who go out of their way to support their peers and offer help without expecting anything in return often find that others are more willing to reciprocate. This creates a cycle of goodwill and mutual support, enhancing the leader's influence within the group.

Liking: We are more easily influenced by people we like. This doesn't mean you need to be besties with everyone in your company. Leaders who invest in creating positive, authentic relationships with their peers are more likely to influence them.

Peer Influence:

I learned a lot from the book, *The Tipping Point* by Malcolm Gladwell. In the book, he talks about The Law of The few. He breaks that down into three categories of people in any group.

- **The Connectors** – influential type people usually very active in social media and other networks. These are the folks who spread the word about the company, vision, mission, etc.

- **The Mavens** – These are the ones who focus on a specific niche. They love being in the know and being the go- to for resources and answers in the group.

- **The Salesmen** – These are the people who champion an idea or product. They have the power of persuasion and the skill to convince other people of the benefits of the organization or the mission and vision.

I want to focus here on the Mavens or what is referred to as the middle bench. These folks work directly with the front line. They are the leadership liaisons who can tilt the communication to go up or down. They can make or break you. The Mavens have the power to influence the other members of the group, and they can affect people, opinions, and the overall energy of the organization. As a leader, it's your responsibility to teach leaders to be leaders. Peer influence is such a strong component of leadership up and down the line.

In my company, Maven is the mentor teacher. Our hierarchy is:

- **Assistant teacher** – helping the lead teacher

- **Lead teacher** – most of our teachers working in their classrooms

- **Mentor teacher** – Teachers in the classroom, but also responsible for onboarding new teachers, mentoring all new teachers coming in, and being the go-to person for all our teachers when they have questions or need resources and help.

- **Team lead, Curriculum Coordinator, Behavior Support, Education Coach** - also teachers but supervises the mentor teachers

- **Directors** – they do not teach in a classroom but run the building and report to their regional

- **Regional and Department Directors**- they oversee several locations and ensure quality and accountability.

- **Executive Team**

Admittedly we are atypical of the structure other schools like ours utilize. In fact, I teach a whole course on the middle bench with tools and checklists to mastering mentorship that will strengthen the middle bench in any organization, not just schools.

Studies done in both 2022 and 2023 showed that the more successful Fortune 500 companies have a mentor program in place in the company. It's the missing piece. Onboarding is important. We didn't use to have that in child care. Training goes just so far. You need continuing assistance from the middle bench Mavens. Mentoring and coaching have real life applications as well. When things come up, you need internal continued support for the staff in any business.

Now, let's pivot to an arena that has transformed the way we think about influence: social media. Social media influencers have perfected the art of playful influence. They've figured out how to connect with people on an emotional level, creating a sense of joy, fun, and relatability that draws people in. I want to buy everything they promote! And their influence is immense because they don't rely on authority (remember I hate that word)—they rely on connection, playfulness, and authenticity. As leaders, we can take a page from the social media playbook.

Playfulness is a powerful tool for influence, allowing me to connect with my team in ways that are meaningful and fun. Much like social media influencers build a community around their brand, leaders can build a community within their organization. Our "tribe" is a community built on shared values, passion, and playful influence, where everyone feels they belong and can thrive. Influence is a ripple effect, influence doesn't stop with the leader. It ripples outward, touching everyone in the organization. I like to say we bleed from the top, bottom, and inside out. Meaning, when leaders influence their peers, they, in turn, influence those around them, creating a culture of shared responsibility, trust, and collaboration. Our Mentor Teachers have as much influence on the organization as our directors do because they are directly shaping the experiences of those on the front lines. This peer influence is crucial to creating a culture where everyone feels empowered, supported, and motivated to succeed. Mentors are a missing piece for so many organizations.

Let's use our people, our greatest assets to help spread positive influence and magic throughout our companies to create a movement for change.

Intentional Influence Framework for Leadership

This framework was designed to help Discovery Kidzone leaders intentionally choose who influences them and how they, in turn, influence others. By using our core values and becoming mindful of these influences, DKZ leaders can build stronger, more authentic leadership practices that align with their values and goals. This tool encourages self-reflection and strategic action to ensure your leadership is intentional, effective, and aligned with your purpose.

Though created for DKZ, it is applicable to anyone in a leadership role or aspiring to be a leader.

Step 1: Identify Your Influencers (Input Influence)

Instructions: Recognize the people, experiences, or sources that shape your leadership style and decision-making. Evaluate whether these influences align with your values and leadership vision.

Influencer	Positive Impact	Negative Impact	Aligns with My Values & Goals? (Yes/No)	Action Plan (Keep/ Adjust/ Remove)
Example: John Maxwell's 5 Levels of Leadership	*Clear leadership growth framework*	*None*	*Yes*	*Keep and deepen learning*

Reflection Questions:

Are my current influences inspiring me to grow as a leader, or are they holding me back?

_____

_____

Do I need to seek out new influences that align more closely with my evolving leadership vision?

_____

_____

Step 2: Clarify How You Influence Others (Output Influence)

Instructions: Reflect on how your leadership impacts your team, peers, and organization. Consider whether the influence you exert is aligned with your desired leadership identity and values.

Audience/ Group	Key Ways You Influence Them	Desired Influence	Aligns with My Identity? (Yes/No)	Action Plan (Enhance/ Modify/ Reduce)
Example: Leadership team	Encourage collaboration and playful problem-solving	Inspire confidence and innovation	Yes	Enhance by sharing more success stories

Reflection Questions:

How do my actions and behaviors influence those I lead?

_____

_____

Does my influence support my team's growth and align with the culture I want to cultivate?

_____

_____

Step 3: Set Your Leadership Influence Goals

Instructions: Based on the insights from Step 1 and Step 2, set clear leadership influence goals to intentionally shape how you are influenced and how you influence others.

Goal	Why It's Important	Action Steps	Timeline
Example: Seek mentorship from a leader who exemplifies authentic leadership	*To grow in authenticity and confidence*	*Reach out to potential mentors, schedule meetings*	*3 months*

Reflection Questions:

What leadership qualities do I want to develop or enhance in myself?

_____

_____

How can I be more intentional in influencing others in a way that aligns with my values?

_____

_____

Step 4: Create an Influence Action Plan

Instructions: Take deliberate steps to ensure you are fostering the right influences in your life and positively influencing others. Your plan should be actionable and measurable.

A. Influence Intake Plan

What influences will you seek out intentionally? (e.g., mentors, books, conferences) *Example: Attend a leadership retreat focused on authentic leadership.*

_____

_____

_____

B. Influence Output Plan

How will you intentionally influence others? (e.g., through team-building, communication, leadership style) *Example: Incorporate storytelling into team meetings to demonstrate values-based leadership.*

_____

_____

_____

_____

Goal	Who Will Be Impacted	Outcome	Timeline
Example: Incorporate one-on-one check-ins with team leaders to encourage open communication	*Leadership team*	*Build trust and increase transparency*	*Bi-weekly*

Step 5: Continuous Review and Adaptation

Instructions: Leadership is an ongoing journey. Regularly review the influences in your life and the ways you are influencing others to ensure alignment with your values and goals.

Review Date	What Has Changed in Influences?	Impact on Leadership	Next Steps
Example: 3 months	*Started following new leadership thought leaders*	*Broadened perspective on team dynamics*	*Continue learning and share insights with team*

Action Steps for Building Influence and a Collaborative Culture

1. Fostering Authentic Connections

How often do I share personal stories or challenges with my team to build relatability and trust?

_____

_____

_____

Do I encourage open communication in a way that makes every team member feel comfortable sharing their thoughts and feedback?

_____

_____

_____

How often do I have one-on-one check-ins with my team, and what steps can I take to increase these opportunities?

_____

_____

_____

2. Creating a Tribe Mentality

What symbols or rituals exist in my organization to help people feel a sense of belonging?

_____

_____

_____

How often do we celebrate our shared mission and values as a team?

_____

_____

_____

What additional events or initiatives can I implement to strengthen the connection between team members and the organization's purpose?

_____

_____

_____

3. Incorporating Playfulness in Leadership

How do I incorporate play into my leadership style today? How could I do more?

_____

_____

_____

What team-building activities or fun challenges have I implemented recently to reduce stress and encourage creativity?

_____

_____

_____

What more can I do to create opportunities for playful engagement across departments?

_____

_____

_____

4. Leveraging Peer Influence

Have I identified the "Mavens" in my organization, and am I actively supporting them in mentoring others?

_____

_____

_____

How effective is the current onboarding process, and are Mavens or middle-bench leaders providing consistent support to new team members?

_____

_____

_____

What tools and resources do my Mentor Teachers or key influencers need to better support their peers?

_____

_____

_____

5. Building a Collaborative Leadership Structure

Is the leadership structure in my organization clear, and do all team members understand their roles within it?

_____

_____

_____

What leadership training is available at every level, and how can I ensure ongoing development for leaders across the organization?

_____

_____

_____

How can I improve guidance and support in peer leadership to avoid relying on authority alone?

_____

_____

_____

6. Combating Misconceptions About Culture

How often do I address the culture of our organization openly, and do I make space for addressing misconceptions or rumors?

Am I clear with my team about the inclusivity of our culture, and how can I ensure that people feel drawn to our mission naturally?

What actions can I take to clarify any misunderstandings around our tight-knit culture?

---

7. Teaching Peer Leadership

Is there a formal mentorship program in place, and how effective is it in helping new employees adjust to the organization?

_____

_____

_____

Are Mentor Teachers continuously trained and supported, and do they feel confident in leading others?

_____

_____

_____

What additional resources or guidance can I offer to strengthen the middle bench in my organization?

_____

_____

_____

8 . Celebrating Success and Milestones Playfully

How often do I recognize and celebrate team achievements in a fun, engaging way?

_____

_____

_____

Do I encourage my team to celebrate their own milestones and those of their peers?

_____

_____

_____

What more can I do to cultivate a culture of playful recognition and appreciation?

_____

_____

_____

Sources:

1. Malcolm Gladwell's The Tipping Point Gladwell's insights on The Law of the Few—Connectors, Mavens, and Salesmen—highlight the importance of key influencers in any organization. This framework is critical in understanding how peer influence can shape an organization's culture and success. (The Tipping Point: How Little Things Can Make a Big Difference, Malcolm Gladwell, 2000)

2. John Maxwell on Leadership Influence Maxwell famously said, "Leadership is influence, nothing more, nothing less." His teachings underscore that leadership is not about authority but about how well you can influence others to follow your vision. (Leadership: The 21 Irrefutable Laws of Leadership, John Maxwell, 1998)

3. Robert Cialdini's Principles of Influence Cialdini's research on influence, particularly his work on reciprocity and social proof, supports the idea that playful leadership can enhance peer influence by

creating stronger connections and a sense of belonging. (Influence: The Psychology of Persuasion, Robert Cialdini, 1984)

4. The Power of Play in Leadership Research has shown that incorporating play into leadership strategies boosts creativity, reduces stress, and fosters a collaborative culture. The Harvard Business Review highlights how play can drive team performance and innovation. (Harvard Business Review, "Why Play Is Essential for Thriving at Work," 2016)

5. Mentorship and Peer Influence in Fortune 500 Companies Studies from 2022 and 2023 show that mentorship programs are key to the success of top-performing companies. These programs foster leadership development, enhance peer-to-peer support, and increase employee retention. (Forbes, "How Fortune 500 Companies Use Mentorship to Foster Success," 2023)

CHAPTER 8:
(C) CLARITY AND CAPACITY

From 2017 to 2019, I was broken as a wife, mother, and leader. I failed to build capacity in my life and as a result I was lost and burnt out. Up until that point, my business had been on a constant path of growth, and I was just aimlessly following that path with no vision, no plan, and no idea what the hell I was doing. I got to a point where I felt trapped in my marriage, in my business, and in my life. I got really good at pretending, so good that I even started lying to myself. I had reached capacity as a leader, and I tried to work myself to death to cover up the myriad of mistakes I was making.

I may have pursued what I wanted with more clarity, but the happy go lucky role I was playing disguised my own internal desperation. I had to succeed at creating this perfect family. There wasn't another option in my mind, which brought an enormous pressure to the process and warped my ability to ever be truly content with the results. There was always a new problem I needed to master to prove my worth.

I learned I needed to let the pressure off to create the possibility of succeeding.

Ultimately, I was becoming a less than stellar leader. I had to go back and find my Ruby slippers, reassess my influencers and how I was influencing others, and get back on the *Yellow Brick Road*.

Different levels of leadership creates different levels of capacity. The first step is to assess the level of leadership you are on and what levels you strive to achieve in your career and life.

Levels of Leadership

There are different levels of leadership. When you hit a plateau, just like in business, as a leader, you hit different plateaus of leadership. So, the more influential you become, the more you have to change the way that you lead, which will require you to build your capacity as you get to those different levels.

Sometimes, when we hit a wall, we are at a plateau. If our bodies tell us to stop, we might be run down, catch a flu or a cold, and we have to slow down, sleep, rest, and recoup. That is in a sense a plateau. It could mean that you need a mental health day or long weekend, and that's okay. Plateaus are not bad things, especially if you understand them, realize why you are on that plateau, and what to do next.

It's important to understand where you are on the leadership scale and where you want to go. In his book, *Influential Leadership*, John Maxwell discusses what he sees as the five levels of leadership: **position, permission, production, people development, and pinnacle.**

Level One – Position: People follow this leader because the job requires them to do so.

So, this level is not exactly a leadership position; it's where you have been hired for some kind of management position or appointed to one. It's thought that you have potential to be a leader, and you will likely develop the leadership skills needed to move forward. You're going to learn the rules, the procedures, and the policies that need to be enforced with the people you manage. Not much influence or capacity is needed but to get to the next level, you'll likely need to gain some of both. At this level, the staff is going to follow the person that is managing them because they know they have to in order to keep their jobs. This is the level most people start at. If you want to learn new leadership skills, listen to your mentors and accept feedback readily from your team, staff, and even clients. Do so, and you will be moving toward the next level and building the relationships that will help get you there.

Level Two – Permission: People want to follow you more than have to follow you.

At this level, people like your leadership style, and they want to do the things you tell them to do. You've created some kind of relationship with them. You will want to rely more on interpersonal skills when leading your group or staff. Show the team you value them, you trust and respect them, and they will be much more willing to follow where you lead. At this level, you start to show that you care about teamwork, the culture of the business, and the staff you manage.

Level Three - Production: People follow you because you are making things happen.

This level is about results. You've learned to be empathetic and understanding of the needs of the team, and you have your leadership role down. You can guide your team and your business to success. However, this is the level where people get stuck, where they plateau, because everything they've known in the past doesn't work anymore. So, now it's a matter of, *how do I recreate this position for myself and for my company to move us forward?* And how you become a better leader is by producing those results. So this level is results driven, not position driven.

Level Four - People Development. People follow you because of what you've done to help them grow.

This is where now we're getting to that top of the pyramid, and we're getting back up to that contribution level. Now, we're giving back. This is the level where we're teaching, mentoring, building, and even multiplying other leaders. It becomes part of your legacy in the people you mentor, train, and prepare to be the leaders you put in place and often leave behind to keep up your work.

Maxwell writes that the Level 4 leader spends about 80% of their time coaching and 20% on their personal productivity. So, you become a multiplier. It's that top level of contribution, reaching that top level to where we're multiplying ourselves.

This is a very important level and one where a lot of people reach but go no further. We have the results. We know how to get to the results. And now we figure out how to make other people create all those different results as well. This is where influence really starts to shine. You can't do something that's replicable and duplicatable if you don't influence people. They're not going to do things just because you tell them to.

Capacity building at this level is really figuring out how to be influential. It's not knowing how to do the things. It's not knowing how to reach people. You already know how to do that at this level, but now, it's a matter of how you are going to make that influence really shine. I teach my leaders that they almost have to become an influencer. Look at what influencers do on TikTok and Instagram and other platforms. Why do people want to buy that stupid soap they sell? Why do people want to do whatever these people tell them to? It's because they're influential.

Level Five – Pinnacle – People follow because of who you are and what you've accomplished.

The pinnacle of leadership can only be reached if you have done the work of training other leaders who can reach the higher levels of leadership, and not only replicate what you do, but sometimes accomplish even more than you have. You will have created a new generation of leaders. This is not about your personal ambition. Your true mission is to create and empower new leaders who will, in turn, become trainers themselves. You're creating a cycle of excellence, so that your mission and values live well into the future.

This is the rarest type of becoming a leader. This is that 1% of the population; your high level CEOs and your visionaries. They are well-known for their accomplishments. People are constantly watching them, following them in the media and on socials, asking, "What is this person doing? How many lives have they affected?"

They lead organizations, even empires. They are the big wigs out there, who are leading in multiple locations and arenas. This is the level I am striving to reach, personally.

Be Unapologetically Authentic

Everything starts with your why. You influence from the top down and the inside out. Be unapologetically authentic. Your culture needs to bleed from the inside out. Well, what does that mean? You start with your why. If you're unsure what that is, do the five steps to your why, which I learned from Dean Graziosi.

Your influence grows when you know what your why is and you are actually doing what follows the path to your why. Doing so will fuel your passion and therefore makes you unapologetically authentic. You can honestly say, "You need me. I am helping you, and I'm helping so many other people through you."

That's when you really begin to see that you have influence. And that's when your influence, or your culture, bleeds from the inside out because it becomes contagious.

I think Dorothy wanted to go home because she finally realized home was really important. It wasn't what she thought it was. It was true that she had no parents, but she had her aunt and uncle, and her friends, and that was where the love was. That was where the people were who actually cared about her were. And that's where her heart really was, in her home. And she hadn't recognized the value of it until she lost it. When she couldn't get back to it, she realized the value very clearly. I think a lot of times, we don't understand how much someone means to us, how much something means to us, some place means to us, until we lose it. And then we have to figure out how to get it back.

And it's not always easy. And sometimes we never get it back. Knowing that it's important and it equates to knowing your why. Without your why, when you lose your why, you lose your way. You don't have clarity. And once you have that why, and you have that influence, then you can lead with more clarity.

I have created a tool for how to intentionally choose who influences you, how you influence others, and how to use that as a marketing plan. Once again, this tool should be revisited often, at least once or twice a year, and should be shared with your staff. Your middle bench leaders and above can work with your staff to utilize this tool as well. In some ways, everyone is a leader of sorts. This assessment can be useful for anyone in any walk of life or position, but it is essential for people in leadership positions or seeking to be leaders in their field.

Collaboration is Key

In each of these levels, especially when you're running a multi-site organization, is the matter of collaboration. It is super important with each of the different levels. I had an experience with one of my directors that showed the essential need for collaboration. This particular director basically ran the school entrusted to her how she wanted to run it. She didn't follow company policy and values and started turning some of our employees in that location against the rest of the leaders in the company. She didn't use her leadership position as a way to develop people or even as a way to take herself to the next level. To move up a level, she would have had to develop the people underneath her, so she could "multiply" herself and create her successors, which would allow her to move up in the company.

This forced me to come in and take the location back from her leadership. I had to rebuild from the ground up. In many ways, it came down to our middle bench in the organization. They got the title, but we didn't train them enough to make them understand that part of what they needed to do was ask more questions. They were supposed to be asking questions and getting feedback, "How am I doing?" Asking the people below them on the totem pole, "How is everything? What do you need? What can I do for you?" They weren't doing that, and that was my fault because I didn't make them understand enough that it wasn't just, "now, you're a big shot," these are the things you need to do. They weren't catching on, or they weren't getting it fast enough, or the information wasn't given to them in a way that they understood it. People understand information in a lot of different ways. For some people, it has to be auditory and others have to have the info written down for them. Maybe they weren't getting the information in a way that was striking them.

The middle bench is and has to be the brand liaisons. Their job is to translate what the leadership expects and wants down to the front lines and vice versa. And if what the front lines are saying is negative, if they are complaining, this information gets stopped up on the middle bench. They begin to fall into agreement with the complaints. They get sucked into the negativity, and it reflects poorly in their leadership. They increase the sentiment of their staff and things escalate.

If you're not taking the issues of the staff to somebody who can fix things or is going to help you, someone parallel to you or above, then you shouldn't be talking about it. And if you don't come up with at least three solutions, I don't want to hear about it. Don't come and puke your problems on me and then run away. This behavior nearly ruined one of my locations. We flipped it around, but it took all hands on deck to do so.

Leadership Lessons and Responsibilities

The good part of that story is that I had to go in myself and be a director again, be a teacher again. Everybody whose last name was Supalla had to strap on an apron and get their butts in there, even the seven year old!

Where do I need to build capacity in order to get that clarity?

Answering that question is how you push yourself to grow to the next level of leadership. Training, learning, and growing.

We pick a word of the year for the company and the word of the year is what we base all of our company planning on. Our training, our marketing, our community events, our parent events, our everything is based on that word of the year. We break it down into quarters, we plan out the whole year, and then we plan out each quarter, even our staff appreciation; everything. Our word of the year keeps us on track personally too and moves us forward.

The word of the year for the company does the exact same thing as it would for us as an individual. And it's really crazy and great. Our company word this year is *align* because we are having all these acquisitions, and we want to align every person who is already part of the company and all the new people and all the new companies to one vision; one plan.

Be Unapologetically Authentic and True to Your Why

Everything starts with your why. You influence from the top down, inside out. Be unapologetically authentic. Your culture needs to bleed from the inside out. Well, what does that mean? You start with your why, and do the five steps to your why, which I learned from Dean Graziosi. Use this form below and answer the questions. I think you will find it to be very useful in identifying your true why and will give you clarity on this subject. Refer back to it now and then. Our why can change when we experience life changes like getting married, having children, moving to a new place, the death of a parent or many other things that happen we may or may not have control of.

Your influence grows because you know why you actually are doing what you're doing. Your why is what fuels your passion. Knowing your why helps to make you unapologetically authentic because you're like… *"You need me. I am helping you, and I'm helping so many other people through you."*

That's when you really have that influence. And that's when your influence, or your culture, bleeds from the inside out because it becomes contagious. Somehow, this makes me think of Mary Poppins. She's Practically Perfect in every way, and she influences everyone around her. She creates a culture in the home and with the families she takes care of. She changed everything for the Banks family, and they changed from the inside out as well because of her influence on their lives and behaviors.

Without your why or when you lose your why, you lose your way. You don't have clarity. And once you have that why and you have that influence, you can lead with more clarity.

Be clear about your why and use the tool on page 130 as well.

5 Steps to WHY

Ask yourself the same question five times to find out what your why is and if it aligns with your values. For example: Why did you start your center?

Question one	How it motivates me
Question two	How it brings me focus
Question three	How it makes me magical
Question four	Who are you going to impact by what you do?
Question five	Why is this so important to your purpose?

The 5 Steps to WHY
DEEP DIVE TOOL

A Second Tool for Uncovering & Strengthening Your Why

Your why is your foundation—your guiding light that fuels passion, decision-making, and leadership. This tool takes you through five steps to uncover, refine, and reinforce your why, ensuring it remains a powerful force in your journey.

Step 1: The Reflection Why – What started this journey?

- Think back to when you first had the idea, the dream, or the calling that led you here.

- Ask Yourself:

  - *What inspired me to step into this role, this mission, or this business?*

  - *Was there a defining moment that sparked my passion?*

  - *If I could go back and talk to my younger self, what would I say about my purpose?*

Step 2: The Impact Why – Who benefits from your why?

- Your why isn't just about you—it impacts the people you serve, your team, your community.

- Ask Yourself:

- *Who am I making a difference for?*
- *How do my actions, leadership, or services improve lives?*
- *If I stopped doing what I do, what would change for those I impact?*

Step 3: The Alignment Why – Does my why match my actions?

- Sometimes, we get caught up in tasks and lose sight of our true purpose. This step ensures alignment.

- Ask Yourself:

  - *Are my daily choices and priorities reflecting my why?*
  - *What aspects of my work feel in flow with my purpose? What feels misaligned?*
  - *What adjustments can I make to ensure my why stays at the forefront?*

Step 4: The Fuel Why – What keeps me going?

- Every leader faces challenges—your why is your fuel during hard times.

- Ask Yourself:

  - *What keeps me motivated when I feel exhausted or discouraged?*
  - *How do I recharge my passion and energy?*
  - *What rituals, habits, or mindset shifts help me stay committed to my why?*

Step 5: The Future Why – How does my why evolve?

- Your why grows with you. This step is about envisioning where it leads.

- Ask Yourself:

  - *How do I see my why expanding in the next 3-5 years?*

  - *What new opportunities or challenges will push me to refine my why?*

  - *How can I ensure my why remains strong, adaptable, and inspiring?*

How to Use This Tool:

- **Journaling Exercise** – Write out your responses to each step for clarity.

- **Team Reflection** – Use it with your leadership team to align visions.

- **Check-In Practice** – Revisit these five steps regularly (quarterly or yearly) to ensure your why remains strong.

Rachel Supalla www.visiontreeleadership.com 2024

Back to *The Wizard of Oz*...

Dorothy wanted to go home because she finally realized home was really important. It wasn't what she thought. She had an aunt and uncle who really loved her and all her friends at the farm who looked out for her. That's where the love was. That's where the people who actually cared about her lived. And that's where her heart really was, in her home. They were her why!

She hadn't recognized the value of it until she lost it. When she couldn't get back to it, she realized what she already had. I think that a lot of times we don't understand how much someone means to us, how much something means to us, some place means to us, until we lose it. And then we have to figure out how to get it back.

And it's not always easy. And sometimes we never get it back. So, knowing that is important. Once she realized her why, she was able to influence each of her companions to follow her and to follow their own dreams.

She became a true leader. It's a model for us all as leaders.

Eventually, I realized that you have to figure out what your end game is and why. I thought I had hit a wall, but in reality it was more of a plateau. Plateaus in business or leadership are similar to those you find when climbing a mountain. Perhaps, it might help to think about it the way we deal with weight loss or exercise. We hit plateaus we have to push past. As a business leader, when I hit a plateau, I have to consider what I have to do differently while still keeping the end game in mind. It takes clarity to realize you have hit a plateau and how that will affect your end game.

End Goals Can Change:

Sometimes we think we have an end goal that turns out to just be a plateau on a mountain. Even if it is the top of the mountain, you realize, "Hey, look! There's another mountain over there, and it's even higher. Let's climb that one."

It's not that I became bored with my life or my business, but I had accomplished all my goals; or at least I thought I had. *Now what? This is weird!* Suddenly I had to re-evaluate my goals. I had built all this capacity and didn't know what to do with it. So, I asked Julie, of course. "Try breathing for a bit," she said. "This is what breathing and rest feels like."

If you've hit a wall, you might need to take a nap and be ready to go again. Sometimes my brain just shuts down and I am forced to act like a normal person and take a weekend off. When I do that, my brain comes back on fire and full of ideas. You might be able to relate to this. Once you have clarity again, you can be ready to gain in the capacity department. To build capacity, you need the clarity to know what is acceptable and not acceptable to you. This applies to life and work. There can be no compromising your values. You will regret doing that big time. You need to know what the non-negotiables are for you. Identify your expectations and how much and when you might need to adjust those expectations, but never at the expense of your values. Once you can see the new big picture, you work backwards. The big picture will likely change some like it did for me. That's okay. It's just another plateau or maybe that bigger mountain.

It's the same for your team. They may do all the things asked of them. They know the job. They complete all the chores. They understand the details of what is expected of them, and they accomplish what they're supposed to, but sometimes they lose sight of the big picture. They may have to take a different road to go in the direction you need them to go. As a leader, you need to assure them it's okay to veer off the path and do things differently than the original plan as long as they get to the goal. Remember, it has to have an element of fun, magic, and play, or it all becomes stale and tasks become boring things done by rote.

Once you get to the next level in your business, you likely will realize you have a new mountain to climb and that's good. Your team leaders also get stuck, and they need a new project or purpose. Not necessarily a new mountain but a new climb that keeps things interesting. You may have thought you were at the top, but you come to find it was just a cloud or a rock hiding the top from sight. Once you can see what is above the clouds; you can see the next level. Make sure that your team understands this, too.

If you know anything about mountain climbing or rock climbing, you know Basecamp at Everest is not the top of the mountain, and it is super hard to just get there. Basecamp is where you take a break and prepare for the remainder of the climb. There are levels to everything and just rock climbing, you stop for a minute or a night to rest, but there is still more mountain to climb. You physically and mentally reach a wall. It's the same in business. As you continue to gain clarity, you grow your capacity and vice versa.

4 Steps to Capacity Building:

- Soul

- Mind

- Body

- Emotions

I believe it starts with the soul, meaning first you must know who you are at core. What are your values, strengths, weaknesses, personal pitfalls, and gaps? You need clarity on all of that before you can work on your mind and body because they control your emotions. If you do something that goes against your values, it takes a tremendous toll on your capacity for growth. What is really of value to you? What is valuable and not valuable? Sometimes we have to change what we thought was the right thing to do for the business or even for our lives when we realize it goes against our core values.

We talked a lot about mindset and some of that is dependent on your belief in yourself and your abilities. Learning to deal with your imposter syndrome issues and chasing away the Wicked Witch and her influence over your thoughts will help you when it comes time to control your emotions.

Paying attention to the needs of your body, getting rest, exercise, and eating healthy food will also affect your emotional well-being. If you've ever acted irrationally when "hangry," you know what I mean. Sleep deprivation is a real thing. It cripples your capacity to grow and certainly affects your emotions.

Your emotions are the hardest things to control, so they are the last step in the process of capacity building. Knowing your value, knowing yourself, and taking care of yourself will build capacity for the climb up the mountain or mountains. As a business owner, we have to control our emotions in a lot of situations. There will be days when you just want to sit down and cry! I get it. Sometimes, you will have to face your fears. Success and growth can be super scary. There are more and more people depending on you. Believe me, I know what that feels like. I have 10 schools, staff for each facility, and hundreds of students that count on me every single day. I started with one very small school and each time we grew, I had to gain more clarity on my goals, the big picture and how it was changing, and add to my capacity for growth. I am not complaining. I am blessed, but I know it isn't easy to grow. Even in reaching my initial supposed end goal, I now have to reassess and move forward. It turns out, there was another mountain to climb and I had to get above the clouds to see it.

Reflective Questions:

1. When have you experienced a leadership plateau in your life? *Reflect on the signs you may have noticed (e.g., burnout, frustration, stagnation).*

_____

_____

_____

_____

2. What level of leadership do you currently find yourself at? *Based on the five levels of leadership discussed, where are you in your leadership journey?*

_____

_____

_____

_____

3. **What are your personal and professional capacity limits?** *Consider where you have reached your capacity and how that has impacted your leadership, personal life, and overall well-being.*

_____

_____

_____

_____

4. **How does your current leadership style reflect your "why"?** *Evaluate whether your actions and decisions as a leader align with your core purpose.*

_____

_____

_____

_____

5. **How can you be unapologetically authentic in your leadership role?** *Think about areas in your leadership where you might be holding back or not embracing your true self.*

_____

_____

_____

_____

ACTION STEPS

1. Assess Your Leadership Level:

☐ Take time to map out where you are within John Maxwell's five levels of leadership and identify which specific skills or actions you need to focus on to move to the next level.

2. Create a Capacity Plan:

☐ Develop a plan that includes personal boundaries and professional growth strategies to ensure you avoid burnout and continue to build your leadership capacity.

3. Reflect and Reconnect with Your Why:

☐ Do the "Five Whys" exercise to better understand your core motivations and how they align with your leadership and business decisions.

4. Take a Mental Health Check:

☐ Identify areas in your life where you may need to pause, rest, or take a mental health break. Make these pauses part of your routine to avoid reaching capacity again.

5. Set Goals for People Development:

☐ Start working toward Level Four leadership by identifying potential leaders in your organization whom you can mentor and develop.

CHAPTER 9:

MAGICAL PLAYFUL LEADERSHIP INSPIRED BY THE DISNEY WAY

Growing up, Disney was more than just a vacation destination for my family—it was a place where magic and reality intertwined, creating experiences that shaped my outlook on leadership and excellence. The values I absorbed during these trips laid the foundation for my own approach to business and life.

As an adult, I had the opportunity to revisit Disney from a different perspective—this time as a leader, seeking to learn from one of the world's most successful companies. Alongside Melissa, my Executive Experience Officer, we attended the Disney Institute, eager to bring back insights that could help us grow our childcare company, which at the time consisted of only three small locations.

One of the most impactful experiences during this visit was touring the Disney laundry facility. At first glance, it might seem like an ordinary aspect of park operations, but as we walked through, it became clear this facility was a microcosm of Disney's broader philosophy. The laundry operation was a marvel of efficiency and innovation, with employees deeply engaged in their work, motivated by the sense of pride that comes from being part of something bigger.

This is where I learned how important the big picture vision is.

In the world of leadership, few companies evoke the level of admiration and success that Disney does. They're known for their unparalleled guest experiences and innovation. Disney's approach to leadership is not just a series of techniques but a philosophy that can be adapted to any industry. Disney's way of leadership has not only inspired me but also transformed my approach to leading a childcare company. For me, they are a model of perfectly playful in everything they do and espouse. These principles are universally applicable, and I will discuss how they can be tailored to suit different industries while sharing insights from my own experience.

The Disney Leadership Philosophy:

Disney's leadership model is built on a foundation of clear principles and a relentless commitment to excellence. At its core, Disney's approach revolves around four key pillars:

- Safety

- Courtesy

- Show

- Efficiency

These pillars guide their every decision, ensuring the company remains true to its mission of creating magical experiences.

1. Safety: The Cornerstone of Trust

Safety is not just a priority at Disney; it's a non-negotiable. This principle ensures both guests and employees feel secure, laying the groundwork for trust and loyalty.

In my childcare company, safety is the first and foremost concern, and it is our top core value. We have implemented strict safety protocols, from the physical environment to staff training, ensuring parents can trust us with their most precious assets—their children.

2. Courtesy: Elevating the Human Experience

Courtesy at Disney goes beyond basic manners. It's about making every guest feel valued and respected, which in turn fosters emotional connections and repeat business.

We've embedded grace courtesy into our company culture, which is also a Montessori practice. Every interaction, whether with children, parents, or teammates, is approached with empathy and respect. This has cultivated a warm, welcoming, family atmosphere our families deeply appreciate. We also work hard to cultivate a special DKZ experience similar to Disney. Learning is better when it's fun!

3. Show: Every Detail Matters

At Disney, everything is part of the show. This principle drives an obsessive attention to detail, ensuring that every aspect of the guest experience is meticulously crafted.

We view our childcare classroom environment as a stage. From the layout of classrooms to the way teachers present lessons, every detail is designed to enhance the experience for children and their families. We train our team to "set the stage to engage." This commitment to excellence has set us apart in the industry.

4. Efficiency: Streamlining for Success

Efficiency is about delivering a seamless experience without compromising on quality. Disney's focus on operational efficiency allows them to manage large crowds and complex logistics smoothly.

We have adopted efficient processes for everything from daily routines to administrative tasks and systems. We try to automate as much as possible and have a back office to allow the front lines more face time with the children and team. This not only ensures that the center runs smoothly but also allows our team to focus on what truly matters—providing exceptional care and playful education.

Case Study: Disneyland Paris and Leadership Adaptability

One of the most instructive examples of Disney's leadership in action is the case of Disneyland Paris. When the park opened in 1992, it faced significant challenges, from cultural misunderstandings to operational difficulties. The way Disney leadership responded to these challenges provides valuable lessons for any industry.

Cultural Adaptation:

Initially, Disneyland Paris struggled because the American-centric model didn't resonate with European guests. Disney's leaders quickly realized that to succeed, they needed to adapt their offerings to better align with local tastes and preferences. This involved changes in everything from food options to employee training.

Financial Restructuring:

Faced with financial strain due to lower-than-expected attendance and higher operational costs, Disney leadership had to renegotiate debt and revise their financial strategy. This adaptability and willingness to reassess their approach were crucial in turning the situation around.

Long-Term Vision:

Despite the challenges, Disney remained committed to its long-term vision for Disneyland Paris. They continued to invest in new attractions and improvements, which eventually led to the park's success.

In my childcare company, we've faced our own set of challenges, particularly when it comes to adapting to the diverse needs of our community. Inspired by Disney's approach in Paris, we've made a conscious effort to tailor our programs to reflect the cultural values and expectations of the families we serve and adapted based on the culture of each region. This has not only helped us overcome initial hurdles, but also strengthened our relationship with the communities we serve.

Measuring Success: Disney's Metrics for Guest Satisfaction

Disney's commitment to excellence is measurable, and they employ a variety of metrics to ensure they are meeting—and exceeding—guest expectations. These metrics provide a blueprint for how any company can monitor and improve its performance.

1. **Guest Satisfaction Index (GSI):**

   Disney uses GSI to capture comprehensive feedback from guests, combining survey results, Net Promoter Scores, Customer Effort Scores, and real-time feedback. This holistic approach allows them to maintain high standards and quickly address any issues.

2. **Social Media Monitoring:**

   Disney actively monitors social media to gauge public sentiment. This not only helps them stay connected with their audience, but also allows them to respond promptly to any concerns or trends.

3. **On-Site Observations:**

   Disney's Cast Members are trained to observe guest behavior and interactions, providing real-time insights into the guest experience. This data is used to make immediate improvements where necessary.

4. **Service Recovery Metrics:**

Disney measures the effectiveness of their service recovery efforts, focusing on how well they can resolve issues and turn around a guest's experience.

We have adapted these metrics to fit our context. For instance, we use parent surveys and direct feedback mechanisms to gauge satisfaction with our services. We also monitor social media channels to stay in tune with our community's needs and preferences. Additionally, we place a strong emphasis on service recovery, ensuring that any issues are resolved quickly and to the satisfaction of our families. We have scorecards for every member of the team to ensure accountability.

SWOT Analysis: Disney's Strategic Tool (Strengths, Weaknesses, Opportunities, Threats)

Disney's use of SWOT analysis is integral to their strategic planning process. By identifying their Strengths, Weaknesses, Opportunities, and Threats, Disney ensures that their strategies are both proactive and resilient.

- STRENGTHS: Disney's brand power and diversified portfolio are among their greatest strengths, allowing them to leverage their reputation and resources across multiple markets.

- WEAKNESSES: High operational costs and over-reliance on the U.S. market are areas of vulnerability that Disney continuously addresses.

- OPPORTUNITIES: Emerging markets and digital transformation represent significant growth opportunities Disney is actively pursuing.

- THREATS: Economic downturns and competition are ongoing challenges that require careful navigation.

Strategic Decisions Using SWOT:

One of the ways Disney has successfully used SWOT is by expanding into international markets, such as the opening of Shanghai Disneyland. This move was driven by the recognition of opportunities in Asia and the need to diversify beyond the U.S. market.

In our company, we regularly conduct SWOT analyses to inform our strategic decisions for each location. For example, recognizing the opportunity to expand our services to meet the growing demand for infant care, we invested in specialized training and facilities to cater to this demographic. This decision was guided by our SWOT analysis, which highlighted both the opportunity and the resources we had to capitalize on it.

Strategic Planning: The Disney Way

Disney's approach to strategic planning is a model of long-term vision, data-driven decision-making, and stakeholder alignment.

1. Long-Term Vision:

Disney's strategic plans are built around a long-term vision, often spanning a decade or more. This forward-thinking approach allows them to remain leaders in their industry while continuously innovating.

2. Data-Driven Decisions:

Disney relies heavily on data and research to inform their strategies. This ensures that their decisions are grounded in reality and can adapt to changing circumstances.

3. Stakeholder Alignment:

Ensuring that all stakeholders, from employees to partners, are aligned with the strategic vision is critical to Disney's success. This alignment is maintained through clear communication and a shared commitment to the company's goals.

4. Innovation and Creativity:

Disney's culture of innovation is integral to their strategic planning. By fostering creativity and encouraging risk-taking, they continuously push the boundaries of what's possible.

5. Execution and Accountability:

Disney's strategic plans are broken down into clear milestones, with specific metrics to track progress. This ensures accountability and allows for adjustments as needed.

We've adopted a similar approach in our strategic planning. By setting a clear, long-term vision and using data to guide our decisions, we've been able to grow our company sustainably. Our focus on innovation and the DKZ way, whether through new programs or enhanced facilities, has kept us ahead of the curve. Additionally, we ensure that all our staff are aligned with our strategic goals through regular communication and training.

CHAPTER 10:

LEAVING A LEGACY
OF LEADERSHIP

A Leadership Lesson – Acquiring New Schools

Recently we acquired three schools in the Bozeman Montana area. It was a difficult transition due to different leadership styles and expectations. Moving from the style of hands-off leadership to our style of accountability leadership caused some serious flack. The folks running the schools from directors to teachers had low accountability, and they were all pretty much all operating on their own. We are talking about roughly 40 teachers and about 120 kids. There was a leader at each location and a Regional Director, but I could not get buy-in from most of them. To stay with my metaphor, in fact, to them, I was like, this big, corporate wicked witch, yes, the actual Wicked Witch, coming in to totally change their way of doing things, and they were very comfortable with the status quo.

I brought my leaders from Helena, because my leaders in Helena are fabulous and have been with me forever. They get why we do things the way we do and know, firsthand, why our systems of accountability work. They went to work trying to help the staff of these three schools adapt to our systems and goals. But I'm sure they saw these leaders as my little flying monkeys, so it took a really long time to get them to align with our team.

Overall, the families were pretty good with the changes. Bozeman, Montana is a very exclusive and affluent community. Celebrities and famous business notables live there, and in fact, Bozeman boasts the most billionaires per capita of any city in America. However, the teachers in Bozeman were so used to doing things their own way that it was a real uphill battle to get them to change. Bozeman has a different demographic. It's almost like Los Angeles and people often move to Bozeman from California. It's very tec- heavy and something like 60% of people in Bozeman work remotely, because their businesses are worldwide and they do business all over the world. Due to the demographics and overall affluence of the communities, teachers in those schools had different expectations. They were among the highest-paid educators in my network and understandably wanted to maintain that level of income. However, balancing competitive compensation with clear expectations and accountability was a challenge.

I found myself stepping on eggshells acquiescing to them.

"Okay, we'll wait for cameras," I agreed, because they didn't want cameras.

"Okay, we'll wait on having teachers wear our branded shirts at school." We have shirts with our logo and school colors. They didn't like them, so we let them wait on wearing the shirts for a bit.

I was agreeing to things so as not to rock the boat.

"Okay. We'll wait for whatever on… just all the things."

Finally, it slowly got to the point where I started to push back on important rules.

"Okay, you cannot have your cell phone in the classroom. That's a safety issue. So, we have to put the cell phones away."

They complained that there wasn't a secure place to keep their phones, so I bought them lock boxes.

"Okay? You can put your cell phone in a lock box. You take the key with you. It's secure."

No matter what the issues, there was always pushback on everything. When it came to cameras in their classrooms, they said, "You're going to micromanage us!"

My answer was, "Well, the cameras are coming, and it is for your safety, the children, and the parents."

I had to spoon-feed them one thing at a time and slowly it started to get better.

We acquired the Utah schools we had wanted to purchase around the same time, and they were going great. Everything was great… for a while. Around the beginning of summer, all of a sudden, the shit hit the fan.

I thought, *what is happening?* We got a random email from a fake person, a fake "member of the community," but it was actually a staff member. I don't know who it was to this day, but it was basically listing all of the things we've done wrong and complaining that we don't listen to the staff. Mind you, when we bought the schools, we raised the pay scale, added bonuses, added more benefits, and bought tons of new materials and supplies. We implemented our well-tested systems that make things easier for our staff members and allow us to offer a better experience for our students and their families.

This all blew up because we were having our staff retreat the following week after receiving the email. My dream was to have all three school regions meet somewhere in the middle, so that we could all be together for one day. I was paying all their expenses. They got 16 paid hours of professional development. We had speakers coming in, food, swag, gifts, and prizes. This was a big thing, and I wanted it to be really fun.

Bozeman lost it over having to participate. They complained, "I can't believe you're making me go to this and I have to drive there. It's three and a half hours away." The schools would be closed for those three days so that they could go to the retreat, and they would not get paid if they didn't go to the retreat, but they would get paid and get all those other things for attending.

"If you just want to stay home and don't go to the retreat, you're not getting paid," was my answer. I stood firm.

The email I had gotten from this "Sarah Smith" person was just awful. She claimed that I was in danger of losing my administration. There were two directors during this whole time who had given the most pushback. In childcare, staffing is our biggest expense, and it's based on enrollment. So, if our enrollment is down, we simply need less staff. Enrollment is 50-60% of our revenue. So, if our enrollment is down, we won't have money left to pay the bills. At one of the Bozeman locations, the enrollment was a little bit down, and the administrator had been allowed to have almost as many staff members as students. I had to fix that by letting a couple of the staff go, and the school director did not like this solution, claiming that I was insensitive and unethical for not allowing people to continue to be employed, despite there being no real work for them.

It came down to one director who would not come around and was influencing the entire staff of all three schools. She was mad about the retreat, mad about the cameras, mad about the cell phones, and that I wouldn't let them have their cell phones during class hours. Those were the three main things that caused her and one other staff member, a teacher, to ultimately leave.

Their leaving turned out to be what it took to right the entire ship. We did have one parent who came at me and said all the same things the two disgruntled employees were saying. He was upset we let some staff go. And I went back to him and said, "We have adequate staff, and these few people that you're concerned about leaving does not reflect upon my character or how well our company is doing. It's sad to see them go, but they just don't align with our company values and vision."

If a factory makes 100 things a day and it takes one guy to make the 100 things, you only need one guy, not five guys. It's mathematics. That's all there is to it.

One great thing about us is that we pay our staff no matter what. When we have 30 families paying tuition, we need teachers for 30 kids not 40. If a law firm loses one third of its clients, guess what? Some law clerks and even some newer lawyers are let go.

Bozeman started out as a pain in my side, but I've learned a lot from it. With mergers and acquisitions, when that happens, everybody has to reapply, and then they decide who they're going to keep, what position they're going to put them in, and all of that. I did not do that because I didn't want to disrupt everything. Maybe I should have done that. This is the part that I haven't figured out yet. Should I have done that and then disrupted the entire operation? It's a little bit more tricky because we've got children and families involved, not just a cold corporation making products.

My only regret is that I waited too long. I let the disruptive employees, who didn't align with our vision, values, and high expectations, stay too long. What I learned is that sometimes you just have to just ride out the storm. In the long run, we did lose a few families who were loyal to those teachers. However, we gained more families, and they see how excellent we are as a company. We only lost the teachers who weren't a fit and didn't live up to our high standards, and the teachers who were a fit are even better now or have been promoted, making it better in the end.

And now I have learned to say, "Y'all, these are our expectations. Take it or leave it, because we are the best and I won't settle for less; the kids deserve the best"

If you can afford to ride it out, the wheat cuts from the chaff. Somehow or another, the people who are supposed to take off, take off. The people who won't or who aren't ever coming on board, are not gonna sit around forever because they don't want to be miserable either. Whatever's making them miserable is going to make them leave on their own. And if you have to fire them, you get to the place where you sit them down and say, "Come on, this isn't working right, for you or me?" Ultimately, I want people to love where they work and if they don't, please go!

That works if you have enough income to cover them for a month or two, but after that, it must get to a point where you have to say, "That's enough." This was a great learning experience. It was just a growing pain, and growing pains are fantastic lessons. I came in like the Wicked Witch to them, but the reality was, I wasn't the Wicked Witch. I was more like Glinda, the Good Witch. They couldn't see that at first but eventually, the staff that stayed got to know me. They got to know the people that had worked with me for years, *my beautiful Munchkins*, and knew what value we bring. They came to know me as a playful leader and to trust my "golden leaders," who have gone through pain and joy and have been with me from the beginning. Once they got it, things got really good for all of us and for our students and families.

Bozeman has come full circle, and I couldn't be prouder of where we are now. What started as a challenging transition, filled with resistance and misalignment, has blossomed into something truly special—something filled with joy, teamwork, and a shared vision for making a positive impact on the children and families we serve.

When we first acquired the three schools in Bozeman, it was clear that there was a disconnect between our leadership style and the culture that had been in place. Moving from a hands-off approach to a model built on accountability and high expectations wasn't easy. Some staff resisted the changes, and a few leaders actively pushed against them, creating unnecessary tension. They clung to the old ways of doing things, mistook structure for control, and let misinformation spread. It was a painful process, but through it all, we stayed true to our mission: to provide the best early childhood education experience possible while building a team that truly believes in what we do.

Through perseverance, we overcame the challenges. We stood firm in our values, and slowly but surely, the tide turned. The staff members who didn't align with our vision made their way out, and in their place, new educators and leaders stepped in—people who get it. People who are excited to be part of something bigger, who love working in an environment where teamwork, support, and passion drive everything we do.

Today, Bozeman is thriving. The energy in our schools is completely different—it's vibrant, positive, and full of purpose. We have a team that isn't just showing up to work but is fully engaged, connected, and committed to excellence. Our new leaders have embraced our playful leadership philosophy, and our teachers are not just meeting expectations but exceeding them. They know that accountability is not about micromanaging—it's about creating a workplace where everyone can succeed together.

And the families? They feel it too. The ones who stayed with us through the transition have seen the transformation firsthand. New families continue to join us because they can sense the difference the moment they walk through our doors. They see happy, engaged teachers who love what they do. They know their children are in a place that is safe, structured, and filled with warmth. They trust us.

The best part? We now feel like a true team. It's no longer "us versus them." We have built a culture where our leaders, our teachers, and our families are all rowing in the same direction, working toward a common goal of making a lasting impact in Bozeman. There's no more resistance, no more unnecessary drama—just a shared commitment to excellence and a genuine love for what we do.

This journey has taught me that real transformation takes time. It requires patience, resilience, and the courage to stand by your vision even when things get tough. But when you push through, when you stay the course, and when you surround yourself with people who believe in what you're building—magic happens.

And Bozeman, right now, is pure magic.

Practically Perfect Comes From Perspective

We don't use the word perfect in my house. I expressed this to my kids from an early age, explaining that nothing is or ever will be perfect and that trying to make things perfect is a foolish endeavor. Perfect teaches us nothing, leaves us no room to grow.

Every time someone says, "Okay, this is perfect," especially one of my staff members, I correct them.

"No, it's practically perfect. We don't want things to be perfect. We don't want to be perfect ourselves."

If we were actually perfect, we would stop learning and growing. And if we are not learning and growing, we are dying. Rather, I encourage my kids, my staff, and everyone in my life to strive for practically perfect, consider what did work, what things weren't quite perfect, and learn from that.

I remind my kids, my staff, and especially the leaders in my organization that it is not always about just the destination. I want them to watch when they focus too much on that. Instead, I ask them to pay attention to the journey. This idea, which my mother often reminded me of, may be part of my fascination with Dorothy and her journey down the *Yellow Brick Road*. Her destination was never really the Emerald City. It was about what she learned along the way, the people she met, the champions who helped her, and the challenges she faced. The journey itself was the real destination.

Every character in that story portrayed themselves as one thing but turned out to be another thing. The Lion pretended to be a mean and scary brute, but he was really a scaredy cat. The Scarecrow believed he was "brainless" and the Tin Man claimed to be without

THE PLAYFUL LEADERS TOOLKIT

a heart. The opposite was true of both of them. We had to see them in action to learn who they truly were. Even the witch makes a comment to Dorothy saying how nice it was of her to, "Visit me in my loneliness." She was indeed lonely, if you think about it. Maybe her meanness was a reaction to her sadness and loneliness. We have to look at things from different perspectives and points of view. The musical *Wicked* looks at the whole story from the other side, like turning the picture upside down.

High performance leaders can experience the fact that it is often lonely at the top. When you're a leader, from some people's perspective–you're the Wicked Witch. What vibes are you giving off to have people think of you that way? How can you avoid that or change their perspective and that view of you?

I saw a little meme where a small child says to her mom, "That person was so kind, Mommy." The mother replies, "Yes, they all are once you get to know them." That's generally true, and even true of the Wicked Witches in our lives. We have to take the time to learn about them, to know what makes them appear as they do or act as they do. We need to take the time to learn about other people in general.

I was recently stuck at the airport, as I often am, waiting for my plane. A gentleman sat down and just started talking to me. We had a whole conversation, and I learned all about him. The time flew by in a pleasant way. It was unexpected. People don't do this kind of thing often enough. We isolate ourselves, stare at our phones, and keep to ourselves. Imagine if we took the time to chat with strangers instead? Who might we meet? What might we learn?

We become more rich and full humans if we take the time to be open and put ourselves out there, ask people questions, listen more, and interact with people, even those we don't know. That includes the Wicked Witches in your life, drop your judgment and see who they really are—what makes them that way, makes them act and speak a certain way. When talking to people, whether you know them, or think you do, or not, don't just look at the ground or even at the destination. You have to meet all the characters on your personal *Yellow Brick Road*. You're missing out if you ignore them.

Learn to ask questions. Too often leaders are misunderstood. People often build instant resentment for people who are "in charge." Leaders and not the big bad witch. They are put in people's lives to teach them and guide them. They are put in their life for a reason, so it would be wise to not just make assumptions.

When you make assumptions, you hurt yourself. Learn to look at things from the other person's point of view. Talking to each other solves a lot of misconceptions and wrong ideas. Be intentional with your words, and if you are about to say something harsh, think about what your words mean and what they might convey. When one of my staff wants to come at something full blast, I say, "Add more fluff! Make it better to swallow." We don't know what is happening in anyone's life. By asking questions first, you can learn what drives them, what fuels them, and what makes them act and speak as they do. You might be surprised by what they're dealing with or going through.

Leadership is about the journey. It's okay to strive for practically perfect, but then look back and look at what you've learned. When we are meeting with someone in my schools who has something they need to express, we use the Zulu phrase, "Sawubona."

A greeting that means "I see you" or "we see you". It's more than a polite greeting; it's a way to recognize the value and dignity of each person. It's also an invitation to be present and witness deeply. A common response to "Sawubona" is "Shiboka", which means "I exist for you."[1]

I see you and I hear you. I feel you. I have extreme ADHD, and I am easily distracted. In fact, we live in a distracted culture. Our cell phones are constantly going off with notifications from emails, calls, texts, and even social media posts. TV, news, and all the noise in the world makes it difficult to focus. We don't see people or hear them fully. I insist that we stop, point our feet toward the person to engage our brain to actively listen to the person in front of us. I want to cultivate this as a culture with my leadership.

My passion is more than to create a great business or buy more schools. It is to create better humans. Being honest, for a long time, my empathy was at an all-time low, and I had a low threshold for hearing people's problems. But I knew I wanted to create better humans and that starts with creating better littles. We have a mental health crisis in America and, in fact, around the world. I believe a lot of mental health issues can be calmed with play. Tom Brady said in an interview recently that excitement fueled him as a player. When he felt gloomy or noticed he was becoming complacent, it negatively affected his game.

Little humans need a happy place to learn and grow and to learn to use their words to express their emotions. It's the same with adults, especially those who never learned this as kids and now have mental health issues. To feel better, in part, means to think better, making it easier to find solutions to problems. In our schools, we call this pattern interrupt. When we have a kid with a behavior issue,

1 *https://www.loominternational.org/sawubona/*

we shake up their brain, often with something playful. Adults need more than that in their lives, too.

I am an overthinker. I spiral. My husband will say, "You're spiraling. Jump up and down, spin in circles, do something silly to break up the thoughts in your head." We may not cure mental health with play, but incorporating play to create an interruption can help break the pattern of the thoughts in the brain. Take a walk or a drive, go swing on the swing set in the park. Tap into your inner child. I'm a *Friends* fan and I remember the episode where Rachel and Phoebe were running like fools in the park. Yes, they looked silly, but they were having a blast. Dance like no one is watching. Just play!

I was very moved by the scene in *The Greatest Showman* where they sing the anthem, *This is Me*. This stood out to me as a leader. Barnum was hated by the whole city. They turned against him because he had all these "freaks" in his show. His entertainers felt inferior when they recognized that people saw them as freaks but they also came to a place where they accepted themselves and were proud to be who they were. They sing, "*I am brave, I am bruised, I am who I'm meant to be, this is me!*"

Leaders are bruised! We have big bruises and we have to be brave. In my opinion, leaders are born. It is what you are meant to be! And if you're meant to lead, you have to step into that power and be brave. You have to follow your *Yellow Brick Road*, wherever it leads, with fierce determination, and if you do, nothing will stop you.

CHAPTER 11

INNOVATION AND MOTIVATION IN PLAYFUL LEADERSHIP

HOW TO RESET WHEN YOU'RE READY TO THROW IN THE TOWEL

L eadership, especially playful leadership, is a balancing act between joy and the immense pressure of responsibility. If you've ever led a team or built something from scratch, you know exactly what I'm talking about. There are days when you're riding high, coming up with creative solutions, and genuinely enjoying the ride. And then there are days when it feels like you're dragging yourself through the mud, every step weighed down by challenges, exhaustion, and that creeping thought: "Maybe it's time to throw in the towel."

Believe me, I've been there—many times. But here's the thing: pressure is a privilege. If you're feeling the weight of responsibility, that means you're in a position to make a difference, to lead others, and to create something meaningful. The beauty of playful leadership is that it's not just about keeping things fun. It's about using that spirit of play to fuel innovation, keep motivation alive, and, most importantly, learn how to reset when you're on the brink of burnout.

Innovation as a Playful Leader

Let's talk about innovation first, because without it, we stagnate. In today's world, if you're not innovating, you're falling behind. But here's the secret that most leaders miss: innovation thrives in environments that are playful, curious, and free of fear. It's not about having the biggest budget or the most advanced technology. It's about creating a space where creativity can flourish, where ideas flow, and where failure is seen as just another step toward success.

When I started my business, I had no clue what I was doing operationally. Let's just call it what it was: a mess. But I knew I wanted to create something different, something better. I wanted a place where children could thrive, and that vision pushed me to innovate, even when I didn't have all the answers. What I've learned over the years is that playfulness is a powerful tool for driving innovation. When we approach problems with a playful mindset, we're more willing to experiment, more open to trying new things, and less afraid of failing. And trust me, I've failed more times than I can count.

There's something powerful about giving yourself permission to fail. So many leaders fall into the trap of thinking they have to get everything right the first time, but innovation doesn't happen that way. Some of the best ideas come from playful trial and error. For instance, when we were trying to figure out how to streamline some of our operations, we threw around every idea we could think of—no matter how silly or unconventional. The solution that worked was a combination of three different, seemingly unrelated ideas. It was playful experimentation that led us there, and that's why I believe playfulness is critical for innovation.

In my business, we've adopted the mentality that every challenge is an opportunity to play and explore new possibilities. This doesn't mean we're reckless—it means we're intentional about approaching problems with curiosity and creativity. I encourage my team to think outside the box, to brainstorm freely without worrying about whether their ideas are "good" or "bad." This kind of playful culture fosters innovation in ways that a rigid, serious environment never could.

When you cultivate a playful mindset, it's amazing how much pressure is lifted. People feel freer to contribute, to take risks, and to offer new ideas. As a result, we've seen some of our most significant innovations emerge from these playful, open-minded discussions. And if an idea doesn't work, it's not a failure—it's just part of the process.

But don't get me wrong—there's always pressure. And that's where you have to remind yourself: pressure is a privilege. It means you're doing something that matters. If you weren't feeling that pressure, you'd be coasting, and coasting never leads to breakthroughs.

Building an Innovative Culture: Playful Tools and Tactics

Innovation as a playful leader goes beyond just brainstorming—it's also about the tools and processes you implement within your organization to foster a creative culture. One of the things we've done at Discovery Kidzone is to incorporate a few practices that promote creativity, encourage experimentation, and keep everyone on their toes in a playful, productive way.

1. **The "No Wrong Answers" Brainstorming Sessions:**

When we're faced with a challenge, I call one of our "no wrong answer" brainstorming sessions where the team is encouraged to share their ideas, no matter how outlandish they might seem. The rules are simple: no judgment and no dismissal of any idea until we've heard them all. You'd be surprised at how many seemingly "crazy" ideas spark real, actionable solutions. It's about giving everyone permission to be bold and creative without the fear of being shot down.

2. **Monthly Innovation Challenges:**

We've also started doing monthly innovation challenges where team members are encouraged to identify a problem or opportunity within their area of work and come up with potential solutions. These aren't formal projects. They're more like playful thought experiments where we celebrate creativity, whether the idea works or not. The goal is to keep everyone thinking innovatively, even about the day-to-day processes we often take for granted.

3. **Celebrate Failure:**

Here's the thing—if you're not failing every now and then, you're not trying hard enough. At Discovery Kidzone, we've learned to embrace failure as part of the innovation process. Every quarter, we hold a "Celebrating Failures" meeting where team members share the projects or ideas that didn't pan out and what they learned from them. It turns the concept of failure on its head and encourages everyone to take more risks, knowing that even "failures" have value.

Motivation and Playfulness: The Heart of Leadership

Now, let's talk about motivation. One of the hardest parts of leadership is staying motivated and keeping your team motivated, especially when things get tough. It's easy to be motivated when everything's going well, but the real challenge is keeping that fire alive when you're facing setbacks, stress, or sheer exhaustion.

For me, motivation as a playful leader comes from remembering why I started. My "why" has always been about more than just running a business. I believe deeply in what we do at Discovery Kidzone. Childcare isn't just a job—it's an extension of the family, a place where children can grow, explore, and develop a love for learning. That core belief keeps me grounded and energized, even on the hardest days.

Motivation, for me, also comes from the team I'm surrounded by. There's something incredibly powerful about working with a group of people who are all aligned with the same vision and who bring their unique strengths to the table. When I see my team excited, engaged, and putting their heart into what they do, it reignites my own motivation. It reminds me we're not just in this for ourselves—we're in it for something bigger. That shared sense of purpose is what keeps us going, even on the toughest days.

The Motivation Cycle: Keeping the Fire Alive

Here's what I've learned about motivation over the years: it's not a constant. It ebbs and flows, and that's okay. There will be days when you're on fire, full of energy, and excited about the work ahead. And there will be days when you're dragging yourself to the finish line. The key is recognizing that motivation is cyclical, and learning how to nurture it when it's low.

One of the ways I keep myself motivated is by breaking things down into smaller, more manageable pieces. When you're looking at a huge project or goal, it can feel overwhelming. But if you break it down into smaller steps, you can celebrate the progress along the way, which keeps the momentum going. I've found that celebrating those small wins—both for myself and my team—is a powerful motivator. It reminds us that we're moving forward, even when the road is long.

For instance, we had a major project recently where we were launching a new program at one of our centers. The amount of work involved was overwhelming, and there were moments when I thought, "How are we ever going to pull this off?" But instead of focusing on the enormity of the project, I broke it down into weekly milestones. Each time we hit a milestone, we celebrated it—whether it was finalizing the curriculum, getting the marketing materials done, or hiring new staff. Those little celebrations kept us motivated, even when the bigger goal felt far away.

Playful Motivation: Creating Joy in the Process

Motivation as a playful leader also comes from finding joy in the process, not just the outcome. I've learned that when you're too focused on the end result, you miss out on the joy of the journey. Playfulness keeps us connected to the fun of what we're doing, even when things are tough.

At Discovery Kidzone, we make it a point to infuse playfulness into our daily work, whether it's through team-building games, light-hearted competitions, or just creating an atmosphere where laughter is encouraged. I'm a big believer that work doesn't have to be serious to be effective. In fact, when people are enjoying themselves, they're more likely to be creative, productive, and motivated.

One of our favorite traditions is the "Fun Friday Challenge." Every Friday, we do something playful as a team. Sometimes it's as simple as a trivia game during lunch, and other times we get more elaborate—like themed dress-up days, scavenger hunts, or even friendly competitions like, "Who Can Build the Best Lego Structure?" It may sound silly, but these little moments of joy bring us together, break up the stress, and remind us that we can have fun while working toward our goals. These activities aren't just about having a good time (though, that's definitely part of it); they help reinforce the kind of innovative, playful culture we've built at Discovery Kidzone.

It's also a reminder that, as a leader, you set the tone. If you're stressed out, anxious, and overwhelmed, that energy trickles down to your team. But if you're playful, upbeat, and willing to laugh—even in the middle of a challenge—that creates an atmosphere where people feel comfortable being themselves, taking risks, and staying motivated. The best part? When your team is happy and motivated, they're more creative, engaged, and productive.

When It's All Too Much: Recognizing Burnout and Taking a Reset

Even with all the innovation and motivation in the world, there are moments when you just hit a wall. You're tired, everything feels like too much, and the thought of throwing in the towel crosses your mind more than once. Burnout is real, and if you don't address it, it can take down even the most passionate and driven leaders.

I'll be honest—burnout has hit me hard more times than I care to admit. There have been moments when I've thought, "What am I even doing? Is it worth it?" And those moments can be scary because they make you question everything. But what I've learned is that those are the moments when it's time to reset. You don't quit—you recharge.

Resetting When You Want to Throw in the Towel

So, what do you do when it feels like it's all too much? How do you reset when you're exhausted, overwhelmed, and ready to walk away? Here's what's worked for me:

1. **Step Away and Gain Perspective:**

   When you're deep in the trenches, it's hard to see things clearly. One of the best things you can do when you're feeling burnt out is to step away, even if it's just for a little while. Take a walk, get outside, spend time with your family—whatever helps you clear your head. Stepping away gives you the space to see the bigger picture and remind yourself why you started in the first place.

   For me, stepping back often involves spending time with my kids. They remind me of the joy in life, the simple things that matter most, and that alone helps me reset. Sometimes, all it takes is a little distance to gain some much-needed clarity. One of my favorite ways to reset is spending a weekend out in nature with my family—getting away from the noise, disconnecting from work, and just focusing on the present. That always brings me back feeling more grounded.

2. **Delegate and Trust Your Team:**

   As leaders, especially entrepreneurs, we often feel like we have to carry everything on our shoulders. But that's not true, and it's not sustainable. One of the biggest lessons I've learned is the power of delegation. You hired your team for a reason—let them help you carry the load. Delegating doesn't just lighten your burden; it also empowers your team and helps them grow.

When I hit that point of burnout, I've learned to trust my team more. It's easy to fall into the trap of thinking you have to do everything yourself, but the reality is, your team is capable and ready to step up. Let them. Trust them. It's not a sign of weakness—it's a sign of smart leadership.

Like I said earlier one of the best things I have done is hiring the right people and putting the right people in the right seats. Delegating key tasks to them has allowed me to step back when I need to reset, knowing that the business won't fall apart in my absence. It's not just about taking things off your plate—it's about creating a team you can truly rely on.

3. Reframe the Challenges:

When everything feels overwhelming, it's easy to see challenges as insurmountable. But often, the issue isn't the problem itself—it's how we're looking at it. One way I reset is by reframing the challenges I'm facing. Instead of viewing them as obstacles, I try to see them as opportunities for growth and innovation.

For example, if we're facing an issue with enrollment or staffing, I'll ask myself, "What can we learn from this? How can we approach this differently?" Shifting my mindset from frustration to curiosity opens up new possibilities and reminds me to approach problems with a sense of play and creativity.

One example that comes to mind is when we were facing a major staffing shortage a couple of years ago. It felt like an impossible problem. No matter what we tried, we couldn't seem to hire the right people fast enough. Instead of getting bogged down by the stress of the situation, we reframed it as an opportunity to rethink how we were recruiting and training new staff. We started hosting fun, interactive hiring events where potential employees could experience our playful culture firsthand. It not only made the hiring process more enjoyable, but it also helped us attract the right kind of people who aligned with our values.

4. Reconnect with Your "Why":

When burnout hits, it's easy to lose sight of why you started in the first place. One of the most powerful ways to reset is to reconnect with your purpose. For me, that often involves visiting one of our centers and spending time with the kids. Seeing their joy, their curiosity, and their growth reminds me why I do what I do. It reignites my passion and gives me the energy to keep going.

I think about all the families we serve, and it brings me back to that core belief: childcare is an extension of the family, and all children deserve a safe, nurturing environment where they can explore and develop a love for learning. That belief is what drives me, and when I'm feeling drained, reconnecting with it helps me refocus and reset.

5. Be Kind to Yourself:

Lastly, and most importantly, be kind to yourself. Leadership is hard, and it's okay to have moments where you feel like you're failing. The key is not to stay in that place of self-doubt. Give yourself permission to rest, make mistakes, and learn from them. You don't have to be perfect—you just have to keep moving forward.

I've had to learn this the hard way. I used to think that being a good leader meant always having the answers, always being "on." But I've come to realize that the best leaders are the ones who are willing to be vulnerable, admit when they need help, and take time to recharge. Being kind to yourself isn't just about self-care—it's about sustainability. You can't pour from an empty cup, so take the time to refill it when needed.

At Discovery Kidzone, we value self-care so much that we give all our leaders a self-care bonus every month to use as they please, whether that's for a massage, a mini getaway, or just something that brings them joy. We also offer mental health services, including therapy, because we know how critical mental health is to being an effective leader. We recognize that for our leaders to give their best to the children and families we serve, they have to take care of themselves first.

Practical Strategies for Recharging and Sustaining Playful Leadership

It's one thing to know you need to reset when things get over-whelming, but it's another to put practical strategies in place to make that happen. Here are some additional tips I've found useful for staying grounded and maintaining playful leadership when life feels like it's too much:

1. Create Space for Daily Reflection:

I've started building time into my day for quiet reflection. It doesn't have to be long—even just 10 minutes of journaling or sitting in silence can make a huge difference. Taking that time helps me clear my head, gain perspective, and refocus on what's most important. It also gives me a chance to check in with myself and make sure I'm not heading toward burnout.

2. Schedule Play into Your Week:

It sounds strange, but scheduling play into your week can be a game-changer. Whether it's a creative hobby, exercise, or just something that makes you laugh, having designated time for play keeps you energized.

3. Build a Support Network:

Playful leadership doesn't mean you have to do it alone. Surround yourself with a strong support network—people who get you, who lift you up, and who can provide perspective when you're too close to the problem. For me, that's my team, my family, and a few trusted mentors. We all need people we can lean on when things get tough, so don't be afraid to ask for help when you need it.

At the end of the day, playful leadership is about balance—between innovation and pressure, between motivation and rest. There will be days when you feel unstoppable, and there will be days when you want to throw in the towel. But remember, pressure is a privilege, and the ability to lead with playfulness is a gift. When it all feels like too much, take a step back, reset, and remind yourself why you started in the first place. The world needs playful leaders now more than ever, and you owe it to yourself and your team to keep showing up with joy and creativity.

CHAPTER 12

CONQUERING THE WICKED WITCH

Strategies for Beating Challenges and Roadblocks in Leadership

As a leader, the journey isn't always yellow brick roads and rainbows (though, wouldn't that be nice?). There are challenges around every corner. Sometimes they're small and manageable, and other times they're full-blown roadblocks that make you feel like the universe is testing your patience. But here's the deal: leadership isn't about dodging these challenges; it's about grabbing your broomstick, staring those wicked witches in the face, and figuring out how to take them down. These challenges are the "wicked witches" of business—the ones that stand in your way, stir up chaos, and make you question whether you're on the right path.

But just like in *The Wizard of Oz*, there's always a way to defeat the wicked witch. It's not always pretty, but when you face obstacles with courage, creativity, and a little bit of playfulness, you'll find no challenge is too big to overcome.

Facing the Wicked Witch: Leadership Challenges

Leadership is full of wicked witches—those metaphorical roadblocks that throw everything at you, from financial headaches to team drama, to sheer burnout. And trust me, I've faced more than my fair share of witches. Sometimes it feels like, just when you've defeated one, another pops up, cackling. Whether it's a tough business decision, a staffing crisis, or an unexpected financial hit, these "witches" can make you feel like you're stuck in a storm instead of leading with purpose. It's enough to make anyone want to hang up their hat for a day and hide.

But here's the thing: those wicked witches? They are there to test you, to push your resilience, your creativity, and your ability to lead. They force you to think outside the box, to innovate, and—most importantly—to lean on your team for support. Every challenge you face as a leader is a chance to grow, even if it doesn't feel like it at the time. Trust me, I know.

In Wicked, Elphaba faces relentless criticism and misunderstanding, despite her best intentions. She could have let the world's perception of her dictate her actions, but instead, she embraced her power, learned from her challenges, and found ways to rise above. As leaders, we face similar pressures. The key is to keep moving forward, even when it feels like the odds are stacked against you.

The Wicked Witch Roadblock Tool: My Story of Facing Challenges

Let me give you a little glimpse behind the curtain—this isn't a theoretical exercise. When we were in the middle of a major expansion with Discovery Kidzone, everything seemed to be going great—until it wasn't. We hit one of those massive roadblocks:

staffing numbers were dropping, enrollment wasn't picking up the way we had projected, and we were bleeding money faster than we could patch the holes. Cue the wicked witch moment.

It felt like everything was falling apart, and that sinking feeling in my gut made me wonder if we had made the wrong move.

I remember sitting at my desk, staring at our financials, asking myself, "How did we get here?" It would have been easy—so easy—to pull back, to go into survival mode, and maybe even scale down our vision. But instead, I developed what I now call the Wicked Witch Roadblock Tool—a method I use to tackle these challenges head-on.

Step 1: Identify the Witch (Acknowledge the Challenge)

The first step to solving any problem is admitting it exists. Pretending it's not there won't make it disappear. In this case, it was clear. We were facing staffing shortages, low enrollment, and a financial squeeze that could've put us under. I had to admit we were in trouble.

Denial only gives the problem more power. You've got to stare that witch down and say, "I see you." In *The Wizard of Oz*, Dorothy didn't shy away from the Wicked Witch—she confronted her head-on. In *Wicked*, Elphaba acknowledges the weight of her struggles, even when the world refuses to understand her. Leadership requires the same courage to confront challenges directly.

Step 2: Gather Your Team of Allies (Lean on Your Team)

Dorothy didn't take down the Wicked Witch by herself, and neither should you. One of the best lessons I've learned as a leader is that you don't have to go it alone.

I called in my leadership team, and we started brainstorming solutions together. We needed fresh ideas—fast. We talked about staffing strategies, new ways to market the center, and ideas to bring in more families. The insights and creativity that came from that team effort? Invaluable.

Just like Dorothy's team—the Scarecrow, the Tin Man, and the Cowardly Lion—your allies bring unique strengths to the table. They help you see the challenge from different perspectives, creating solutions that are stronger because they're built collaboratively.

Step 3: Find the Magic (Innovate and Adapt)

Every roadblock is an opportunity to innovate. And no, that's not just a cheesy leadership line—it's true.

We realized we had to rethink how we were recruiting and retaining staff. We started offering more flexible hours, promoting a better work-life balance, and threw in higher incentives for referrals. We also shifted our marketing strategy to focus more on community outreach and local partnerships.

In Wicked, Elphaba's defining moment comes when she sings "Defying Gravity". She embraces her unique abilities and dares to think differently, even when the world tries to hold her back. That's the essence of innovation: daring to think outside the box and finding creative ways to solve problems.

Step 4: Face the Witch (Tackle the Problem Head-On)

Once we had a plan in place, it was time to act. Facing the witch meant making some tough decisions—cutting unnecessary expenses, reshuffling roles, and working directly with the hiring team to make sure we were filling those positions as quickly as possible.

In *The Wizard of Oz*, Dorothy's bravery in confronting the Wicked Witch teaches us that action is the antidote to fear. As leaders, we have to do the same: take bold, decisive steps to move forward, even when the path feels uncertain.

Step 5: Celebrate Your Victory (Reflect and Grow)

Here's the thing about taking down the Wicked Witch—you've got to celebrate when you come out on the other side.

After months of hard work, we started seeing the results. Enrollment numbers went up, staffing stabilized, and our financials were back on track. But—and this is crucial—taking time to reflect on what we learned from the experience was key.

In Wicked, Elphaba and Glinda's duet "For Good" is a moment of reflection on how their challenges shaped them. Leaders should take a similar approach: celebrate the victories, acknowledge the lessons learned, and use them to grow stronger.

Statistics on Business Roadblocks

Now, let's talk hard facts. You might think your business is the only one dealing with wicked witches, but let me tell you—roadblocks are a universal experience for leaders. According to a study by the U.S. Small Business Administration:

- 80% of small businesses face financial challenges within their first five years.

- 40% of business leaders cite staffing as their biggest head-ache—especially in industries like childcare, where finding and keeping good employees is critical.

- 20% of businesses hit major roadblocks when scaling due to poor planning or limited resources.

- Over 50% of businesses that face financial distress say better risk management could have saved them.

These stats are daunting, but they're also a reminder that challenges are inevitable—and surmountable.

Top 5 Strategies for Conquering the Wicked Witch: A Leader's Tactical Guide

1. CLARIFY YOUR PURPOSE – Stay grounded in your "why."

2. BUILD AN A-TEAM – Lean on the strengths of your people.

3. TURN FAILURES INTO FUEL – Learn and adapt quickly.

4. GET CREATIVE UNDER PRESSURE – Think outside the box.

5. KEEP PLAYFULNESS ALIVE – Use joy to energize your team.

Leadership will always have its wicked witches. But with cour-age, creativity, and a great team, you can rise above. So grab your broomstick and get ready to lead with resilience—one challenge at a time.

CHAPTER 13:
LEAVING A LEGACY OF INFLUENCE AND STRONG LEADERSHIP

As I am writing this book, I'm learning so many new things that affect how I conduct my business and what I want for my legacy. I'm in the middle of retooling how we create the best way for our team to be in alliance. This is a big pain point I've been experiencing, but that I believe alliance is a sticking point for most businesses and business owners. I'm overcoming the problem, but I've learned a lot of tools because of the changes we are making and the growth we are experiencing.

As I always say, we strive for practically perfect. We don't want things to be perfect. We want our team to always be learning and that includes me. In a sense, I'm in the hardest chapter of my life as a leader. This last year, I really needed to reflect on everything I've gone through. I want to tell that story, and I want to tell it in a way that helps people.

I was impressed by the concepts of team building in a book by Donald B. Egolf, PHD and Sondra L Chester, PHD, *Forming*

Storming, Norming, Performing: Successful Communications in Groups and Teams.

Here is a breakdown of these stages:

Forming Stage:

- Adjusting and getting acquainted
- Positive social interaction is key at this stage

Storming Stage:

- True character is revealed
- Conflict arises
- Authority may be challenged
- Overwhelmed feelings about workload surface
- Unsure feelings about position happens

During this key stage, as a leader you must…

- Execute
- Energize
- Engage
- Explain
- Emphasize

The five dysfunctions of a team that can derail a project especially at this stage are…

- Absence of trust
- Fear of conflict
- Lack of commitment
- Avoidance of Accountability
- Inattention to results

The Norming Stage:

- Start accepting each other
- Put differences aside
- Respect authority
- Begin to feel comfortable around one another
- Commit to your goals
- Accept and offer constructive feedback

The Performing Stage:

- The team becomes more fluid
- More responsibilities are taken on
- Enhanced team performance happens
- Full potential is shown
- Differences are now appreciated

As a leader when we delegate work, team members' full potential is shown. This allows members to leave or join, so you can focus on development of the team.

The Final Stage – Adjourning/Mourning Stage:

- Closing

- Project is finished

- Some team members will become sad because of their attachment to the team

As a leader, when the project ends, you must celebrate the end of the project, give feedback and recognition, and give guidance for future projects.

We have been in the **storming phase** and now we're in the **forming phase**, after which we will finally get to the **building phase**. I just think that I forgot about that, and when I was in the storming phase, I forgot that this is just part of the process. And so, I had to remind myself and my team that what we're going through is just part of the process. In the building or in the forming phase, you have to figure out who's aligned with you and who isn't aligned, and that's why you have to let some people go. But you have to align with your own vision and values first, and then you have to form the team that is based around those things you firmly believe in. You cannot form a team based around your vision and values if the members of the team don't want to follow your vision and values. They won't be a viable part of your team and can't be allowed to be part of your team.

So, you have to have that really strong accountability piece and systems in place to make sure that all that alignment is happening.

And you have to figure out how to hire for growth. This is super important. What does that look like? How do you mentor and train for growth? What does the journey you see your team as being on look like? Something I just did with my team is what we refer to as future pacing. I was able to do it with my team at our leadership retreat. I asked them these questions: "Three years from now, what does your role in the company look like? What does the company itself look like? What do you see for the future of the company?" I told them, "I want you to dream really, really big, and then what does that look like for your team?"

And it was amazing, because it was eye-opening for them. Their responses were like, "Oh, my gosh. Three years from now, we can be doing this and this and this and this, because look where we've come in just three years now, where are we going to be in three years?"

That exercise really helped them think about how they could run with the vision. That's really important for that alliance of the team.

Before I had all these acquisitions, I had gotten to a place where I was good. I had what was essentially a self-running company. I had one school at first, then eventually three schools and an operation that ran like a well-oiled machine, so I didn't have to be involved in the day-to-day minutia of running things. Financially, we were good; everything was great. I had an amazing rock star team. But the opportunities to grow kept coming, and suddenly, we had all these acquisitions. Silly me…I just thought it was going to be easy. I thought it was going to be plug and play. When I only had three schools, things were smooth. I could go do what I wanted. People who I trusted were running the show. I didn't have to be too interactive with it. Then, I built another one, and then we acquired three more, then two more, then we added another. As of now, we have 10 total schools with hundreds of employees and students that we serve every day.

Suddenly, I was back in the game full steam. There were many sleepless nights, traveling like a crazy person. There were money issues, cash flow was tight, because we had all these acquisitions and the enrollment in each school was not full. We kept having to fill spots, so we had to get back into the marketing game, too. Everything before all this was just easy.

You might ask me, *"So, why do it?"*

Because of the end game.

My end game is to create a lasting legacy that impacts many children, many adults, and the communities in which they live and work. That includes my team. My biggest passion is to create teams that are in alliance, teams that can serve the most people in the best possible way. And I am determined to have our teams be inclusive and diverse.

We recently had a situation where my daughter was at odds with one of the teachers in one of our newest acquisition schools. My daughter had been driving two hours each way to Bozeman to help out because she's a freaking rock star, and she knew they needed more hands on deck. She's helping fill in wherever she is needed to do whatever needs doing. A teacher went to her director and said, "I don't want to work with Abbie." Yes, Abbie is my daughter, but I don't play favorites when it comes to my business. She is objectively amazing and one of the best people on our team. Having to hear that a teacher refused to work with her, broke my heart. I literally cried when the director brought this to my attention. Abbie has struggled with anxiety her whole life. She struggled to fit in, and she's thriving and as her mom, not her boss now, this hardworking, kind young person was being rejected again. But it wasn't just me as her mom. It was a matter of, *this is not who we are as the company that I built.* I built a company where we accept everybody.

It begs the question, why did this particular teacher not want to work with Abbie? The simple answer was entitlement. She had been allowed to do things any way she pleased for too long. She didn't want Abbie, or for that matter, anyone, to tell her what to do. In my opinion, this is born of sheer laziness. She didn't want Abbie to come into her classroom because Abbie would come in there and do a great job. That might have made her look like a fool and she might have had to work harder and make some changes. It's easier to just go along to get along as she had been doing for quite a while. She didn't want anybody to hold her accountable. But the real point here is that it doesn't matter why she didn't want to work with her. I don't want people in my company that aren't inclusive, open, and willing to work as a team. I accept people of all walks of life. I want everybody that felt rejected, didn't fit in at school, didn't do all that great in school, or any of those things that can happen in life, to come to my company and feel like they have a safe place. I have created a space that gives them the chance to sparkle, shine, and thrive because they feel loved and accepted. So, that broke my heart in that moment, and it was eye opening for me. *Nope, this is not who we are, and we will not accept people that are like that to work for us.*

I could say that this occurred because the teacher resented being monitored by my daughter, the daughter of the owner of the company. But the truth is that this person is simply willful, and having willful people on my staff is unacceptable. To be part of our team, you have to be open to suggestions, change, and possibilities, and someone coming in to work with you who might know some things you don't or who might have some new, fresh ideas. The teacher in question didn't want to have a conversation with me or with Abbie. She could have expressed why she felt as she did. She didn't express things like she was overwhelmed or felt like she was being usurped or even uncomfortable. She didn't initiate a conversation with her director, me, or Abbie to express how things might work better for everyone. She just said, "No, I won't work with Abbie."

Well, this kind of behavior means it's time to say goodbye to a person like that. I'm the leader here and all things fall on my shoulders. Sometimes we have to just say, "This is no longer working for the company. You are not a good fit for the team," and let them go. Sometimes, especially in these days of worker shortages, we let someone remain on the staff or team because we simply have no one to fill their role. That's understandable, but trust me, move on this kind of employee problem as quickly as possible. This kind of behavior spreads and brings the whole organization down. People can begin to believe that the world's not going to go on without them and that they can do whatever they want and behave however they want because you don't have the resources to fire them and get someone to replace them. No one is irreplaceable! NO ONE!

As a company, as a whole, we're looking at how to best create an alliance of the team in a way that is *Practically Perfect*. What I've learned over this last year is what I will not accept, what is not negotiable because I want us to be different. And the biggest thing is wanting to be a place for people to thrive and grow. Children, yes, of course, but also adults. I want our teachers to feel accepted on our team, even those who were rejected in school and in life. I want them to come here and to feel safe. I don't accept drama. I don't accept gossip or rudeness. Those things are unacceptable. I also include not allowing for laziness in my non-negotiables too. I'm never going to ask my team members to do anything that I would not do. As a leader, you can't be above anything.

Entitlement is something else we just don't allow for and communication is a must. If you feel so entitled that you don't think you need to be responsive, you are not a good fit for our team. Not communicating is a big one for me. I expect my people to respond in a timely manner. If I send a message, I expect at least a simple response back, like, " Got it." or "Yes, thank you." No ghosting or hiding. It only makes things worse when we eventually do connect.

I have learned how much collaboration plays a part in our success. In fact, I think collaboration is a big key to success with any business.

Bozeman, versus the other regions, in a way, has been my guinea pig, because it was so eye-opening and different from anything I had ever done, and still is to this to date. I work with teams all over the world, and the Bozeman team was the most difficult team I'd seen. Dispensing with allowing entitlement is an important thing. I made it clear that we are here to serve. Our staff and team members are here to serve the children that come to us, and we are here to serve each other. We're here to serve our families and the community. They are not here to serve you. And if you think you are entitled to have the organization serve your needs over the needs of the group, then don't work here. Go work somewhere else. That attitude is not going to work for me.

When we started at Bozeman, they didn't want to wear uniforms, they didn't want cameras, and they didn't want to put their phones away. It was just unbelievable. They didn't want to use the curriculum that we used or even wear our company shirts. I had to make it clear that excellence is not a request it is an expectation because our children and families deserve the best.

"If the DKZ way of doing things is not going to work for you, then you're not aligned with us, and not a fit."

You might find it hard to say something like that to a staff member, but there are times when that is the only way to proceed so that the team comes into alliance and can grow.

Servant leadership is huge for me. We are here to serve. I expect my team members to express this by asking, "How can I serve you?"

Finally, one of my big non-negotiables is beauty. I want things in our schools to be as beautiful as they are functional. I'm really big on the concept that our environments need to be beautiful. They need to smell beautiful. They need to be really clean, not all cluttered and disorganized. Color and texture matter. In our case, we are dealing with children. We want our environment to be pleasant and happy and colorful and have a warmth that makes the children, and our staff, feel like this is their home.

As a leader, you must define your non-negotiables, know your vision and values and live that vision every day. Stay in keeping with your values, so you can create an environment where alignment is a no-brainer. Your team will become in alliance with you and with each other when all of this is in place. Sometimes that means letting some folks go and hiring new people.

Growth is hard, but if you want to be a true influence to others and leave a legacy, you gotta do the hard stuff.

Bozeman held more challenges than I have ever experienced. We wound up having a 99% turnover of staff. We also lost some parents who were influenced by the teachers they had known for some time and were made to feel that the new way we work was not the best way. We even got some anonymous calls falsely accusing us of being out of ratio, meaning they suggested that the ratio of teachers to students was incorrect. The Bozeman teachers wanted to have three teachers in every classroom, which was not needed, and we of course had the correct ratio of teachers to students. That issue was cleared up, but we had to go through an inspection with the state from the accusations. The Bozeman staff had always had things the way they preferred, but that way was unsustainable if we were to meet our goals. We could not and would not simply accommodate them to our own detriment. So, we brought the Bozeman schools into compliance with our other very successful school models and eventually, things settled down and moved in the right direction. It will take time for that school to be in the same place as our other schools, but with determination and by not buckling to pressure, we are on our way there.

CHAPTER 14

UNDERSTANDING THE ROLES WITHIN THE ORGANIZATION

One of our biggest gaps or pain points in our company, which we have worked on every year, is the Assistant Director level. The reason for this is, because at this level of leadership, they get a title. Once they get the title of assistant director, while they can do the work involved, they're not mentally prepared to be a leader. They are lacking some of the emotional intelligence required to handle the new position. So, they become somewhat entitled, and they take this title to equate with a level of power that means they can do things their own way or dictate to the people they are in charge of. No, that's not how we are. We're servant leaders, so teaching that level of directors to be a servant leader has been difficult for us. I have created a solution we are implementing to switch that title to one of coordinators. So, now we've got mentor teachers and then coordinators. The new titles will be things like community coordinator, curriculum coordinator, marketing coordinator, etc. Doing this means they're all working as a team by playing to their particular strengths.

Sometimes it's a matter of the words we use and using the words assistant director, somehow made this level of our team one small step down from the Directors who run the day to day at their schools. Sometimes you have to look at the titles you give things, and being more specific about the parameters of the role you're giving them can really help. You don't want people to stomp on each other. Specificity allows you to bring the team together to be clear about their individual roles and responsibilities, and opens up real dialogue on how to work as a team. I think that's a pretty smart way to build a stronger team.

You also have to take responsibility. In my case, I had to admit that I didn't train these team members enough to make them understand what their roles were and how to behave while in that position.

The title of assistant director was not working. This level of our staff were mentally and emotionally immature and ill-prepared to be a leader. That was on me, to be honest. Part of the problem was that they felt underappreciated. In some of our smaller schools, there was not a lot for them to do other than be second in command and do tasks that the directors didn't want to do or didn't have time to do. Their roles were not clearly defined. Now, looking at these roles as coordinators instead has created a new excitement for this level of our staff. We realized they did a great job while our directors were away for two weeks at conferences and that led us to look at things a little differently. They want to take on bigger and more defined roles. They are excited to be able to contribute more to our growth and success, and they can take on more of the day-to-day responsibilities but for specific things not just leftover and often menial tasks.

In creating these coordinator roles, we base each role on both what our company needs and what the strengths of the individual are. For example, some people are good at social media, community outreach, marketing, events, or family involvement. Defining these roles beef up this level of our leadership bench and now, when top level positions come available, we know there will be more people qualified to move up.

One of the most important things that was missing with this group was me. Now, I am investing more time, money, and effort into that level of leadership. Our top leaders are already fabulous and they get a lot of me, but the next levels down don't get enough of me. Now, I am doing things like taking them to a conference, having coaching sessions with them, adding new resources and training, and just having more time in general with me.

Your Organizational Chart

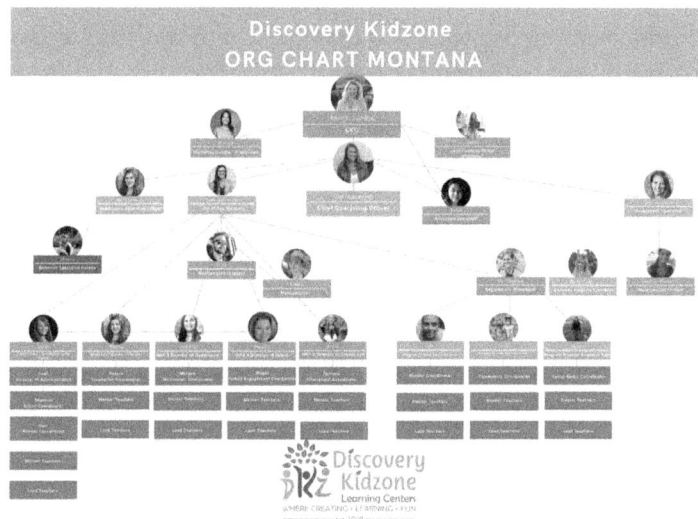

We have a chain of command. If a director is out, the leadership management accountability (LMA) coordinator is the next person to report to. That person will take over the leadership of their school if the program director is out. It is very clear who to report to and when. On the previous page is a breakdown of our organization and the chain of command.

Every company should create an organizational chart. An organization chart or "org chart" is a diagram which is a visual display of who reports to whom and shows the relationship hierarchy of your company. It's imperative to clearly define the structure of a business or any organization. You also need to make clear the role of each individual position on the chart, so there is no question what each person does, what their responsibilities are, and who they report to.

Org charts have many uses which can include as a management tool, for planning growth, or simply as a staff directory of your leadership levels and teams.

In our schools, each coordinator has basic admin responsibilities. Coordinators, our middle bench, are all teachers as well, so most have admin, plus some level of leadership role. There are a few teachers who do not have a leadership role, but they may have a role based on some skill they have and they can do that one thing really well. This helps beef up each department without needing to have a full department. For example, we aren't ready for a stand-alone marketing department yet, but this helps future casts where we are going. As we grow, we will need a full department of marketing. Someone who is a coordinator of marketing will be the likely choice to move into that bigger department if they have shown the passion and skill to do so and want to make that move. We can stay in-house to build that department and other departments that will be needed, and will move people there who really know us and how we work rather than having outsiders coming in with a big learning curve.

As we do this, we see that our people feel like they are a greater part of our growth. They are more passionate about something they are good at and can be useful in that as a coordinator of that role. Some will learn more about strengths they may not have known they had. I have a knack for discovering what seat will work for them and for seeing their potential. I have an eye for this, and I can then move them into the best possible positions. I ask them a set of questions that help me identify what they will be best at. I want to know what lights them up, what is fun for them, and what they are passionate about. Sometimes it takes a little effort to pull this information out of them.

An example of this is one person who when asked about her passion responded with, "I'm passionate about my classroom." In digging a little deeper, she said that her dog was the only thing she was really passionate about. She was a big dog lover. I suggested that she partner with the Human Society. "Why don't you see if we can have the kids go there for a field trip or maybe they can bring us an animal each week." I suggested that at the end of the quarter she then create an event where parents and kids would bring their pets to school and even have rescue folks show up with available pets. She was so excited that she ran with that. She learned she had a strength she hadn't considered.

Big Picture Goals

Each quarter, we do what I refer to as "Picking Your Rock." This concept is based on the idea that you should pick your big rock to fill your jar first so that the smaller rocks will fall into place around it. The target for the company this quarter is enrollment. That is our big rock. Whatever each person on our staff chooses as their big rock should align with their strength, their particular discipline, and align with the company's big rock of increasing enrollment. So, the person who is working on incorporating pet events will think about how that will drive enrollment. Each rock is the big task and must take no more than 12 weeks to accomplish. Then, we have them choose a number—how many people will enroll based on each rock? We base our KPIs on the rocks and check in weekly on progress toward the overall goal.

My personal big rock for this quarter is community outreach. I will accomplish this by writing a series of press releases both about the company and about me and my personal accomplishments. I will also write articles for the local parenting magazine. Next, I will reach out to create more corporate partnerships. Local corporations partner with us to save spots for their employees. They buy spots for employees who have children they would like to enroll in our schools in the future. They then partner with the employee (pay some of the fees as part of their salary, etc.) We save the spots for new parents or employees that are moving to the area to work with them, or employees that are simply seeking a new school for their kiddos. This helps with their staff retention. People are more likely to stay at a company that makes it easier for them to have their children have a good education and especially with newborns. We take kids at six weeks and over, making it easier for them to get back to work sooner. This is done with schools in big cities, but not in our area, and we want to be a cut above.

The main takeaway here is to know the best places for each team member, to create a chart of those roles, and clear definitions of each role. Working with people to see their strengths and making them feel like they are valued, appreciated, and allowed to be creative in ways that speak to their passions will make for a stronger organization. It will also make you a better leader when you lead from this point of view.

MY LEGACY EPILOGUE

I am so incredibly grateful for my life. I am overcome with gratitude as I sit here on my deck at the lake and reflect on how blessed I am. Listening to the birds sing and feeling the warm sun and the wind sweep softly through my hair, makes me realize how much God has given me. The lake is my happy place; it is where I go to ground my spirit and my soul. I can sit in total silence and watch the water playfully ripple across the lake, making different patterns and colors as it interacts with various boats and animals. When a fish jumps, the water encircles the fish as if to hug it and protect it, making the fish feel safe and at home. The different boats create wavy patterns as they pass through, as if the lake is giving a running high five or wave, saying, "Welcome to my home, come play." The smooth stones excitedly dance across the surface until they find a place to dive in and settle. In calm waters, the lake beautifully reflects the majestic mountains and clouds above it. Because the beauty is so vast, the lake feels the responsibility to mirror the beauty to make it spread. The lake is like the best leader you have ever had the pleasure of meeting. It grounds people, is safe and welcoming, playfully connects with visitors, and mirrors and reflects others' beauty and talent to make them shine. I strive to be like the lake as a leader.

Recently, I got to spend a lot of time at the lake with my grandma. She's 85 now, and she is just amazing. She dances with abandon, lives on her own, does everything the way she always has as if time didn't have much effect on her. She does her makeup and her hair every day. She's simply great! During her visit, we were at the lake house and a song that she loved came on. There she was, dancing around in our yard at the lake singing along with the radio.

If you have a chance, take it. If you have dreams, make it.

I was just overcome with emotion watching her. She's always been my hero. She grabs life and just lives it to the fullest. She kept saying, "You can't let the old man in." *I always want to be like you,* I thought.

My husband Eric's grandma is only a couple years older than mine, but she's like, *way* older. You know what I mean? I was discussing that with my grandma, and wanted to know why they were such different people when they were actually so close in age. Once again, she said, "It's because you can't let the old man in." And I thought how proud my grandpa would have been in that moment watching her at our lake house, because that's always been a dream for us to have a lake house, and what a beautiful legacy they started that led me to where I am today. What a joy it is to be able to have this for her, for my family, my kids, and soon, my grandchildren. None of it would have happened without their love and support, their guidance and the gift of knowing how to, "not let the old man in." Playful living is in my bones. It's in my genetics, and it is part of the legacy of my family. My brother, Danny, and I were best friends growing up, and we had a playful relationship that I want for my kids and his kids. We are passing this on to my kids but also to the people at the schools I own. The teachers, the administrators, and the entire staff know that this is my way of living, learning, and teaching. It runs downhill to the students and families we serve. We are creating a huge legacy of joy.

My grandpa was a very playful, loving leader, and my grandma would always play with us as kids, too. During her visit, my grandma started to say that the one thing she regrets in her life was not ever having a career because she was a mom and a grandma her whole life. But then she went on to say, "But I'm not sorry for it." I am so pleased that she will be able to read what I have written about her in this book. I want her to understand that even though she didn't have a career, she was still a leader, and she still continues to leave an incredible legacy every day in everything she does and everything she is, and that's a really important thing. My grandma never yelled at us or made us feel inferior. She was also a playful leader of her family.

My mom plowed through years of trauma and disparagement, so much that it wasn't until I was older and looked back that I realized how much trauma she had being a teen mom married to a drug addict, an alcoholic, and abusive husband, another husband who decided to change his gender, and then another alcoholic husband. She had a baby, my sweet baby sister, Kelly, who died at three months old. She's been divorced four times, but yet she is full of life and magic. She has incredible passions and is creative and unbelievably hardworking. I get my magic and work ethic from her. She's also a playful leader, and she is the one who's constantly reminding me to put my family first and to not work too hard and to not take my family for granted. My sister, Heidi, is also incredibly artistic and creative and has a very imaginative soul. My father, who adopted me, Steve, is extremely charismatic, giving, and magnetic. People just want to be around him and his wife, Kristi.

All these people in my life are a huge part of my legacy. When we're talking about legacy, all these people gave me an incredible love of people and hospitality. They taught me to invite all people in and give them a sense of home and family, even the ones who are lost. They are also the playful leaders for their family and their church, and have taught me the importance of servant leadership. They invite everybody to the table, just like Jesus would have. My in-laws came into my life when I was only 14. That is when I fell in love with my husband. I was a spunky, somewhat unruly, teenager up until that point in my life. They gave me purpose and they grounded me. That is where my love of teaching and leadership began. My mother-in-law gave me an opportunity to teach at a girls' church class. At age 16, I fell in love with teaching the Bible to these young girls and serving the church. I had the opportunity to work alongside some of the best leaders I've ever met.

My in-laws taught me commitment and consistency, and discipline, which are all things I had lacked in my own life growing up. They are the most committed and dedicated humans I know. They will help anybody. If someone needs help, they're always the first to show up. In fact, when I started my schools in 2009, my mother-in-law was my very first employee. We taught preschool together, and to this day, she occasionally will sub at the schools and brings her Mary Poppins bag full of joy and play. My mother-in-law is definitely a playful leader.

I guess what I'm getting at with all of this is that I hope you take the time to reflect on what made you the leader you are. Who are the people in your circle? Who are the people you met growing up, who have been your champions? Who has guided you, and what will your legacy look like? What do you want to be remembered for?

There are many components and attributes needed to make up a good leader, but I believe, with my whole heart, what differentiates you between a good leader and a fabulous, great leader is making the commitment to be a playful leader.

My children are almost all grown now as I write this book. Abbie is 22, Allie is 20, Zack is 18, and Trenton 16. As I think about the future of my legacy, I look at all of them. Abbie told me, the DKZ (Discovery Kidzone) experience is her gift, teaching her to be a playful leader and that when things are hard, to stop and play. Play with your team. Put your work away and play with your family. Allie exudes magic, like her mama and her grandma. She makes everything she does magical, and she wants the world to be a more fun, loving place for everyone. Zack is a sweet, kind, humble, and empathetic friend like my brother and my grandpa. His presence is invited by people all around him who want to know him, sit with him, and talk with him. He listens to them with his whole heart. Trenton is the charismatic, magnetic, and influential one like his mama and grandpa. He's also got a heart on fire for Jesus and serving others. My husband, Eric is the best father, husband and friend I could have ever dreamed of. He would do anything for his family and works harder than anyone I know. He is the reason for it all.

I am still growing as a leader. I am still pretty young in the scope of things, and I hope that I will always seek to grow my leadership skills and remain a "playful leader." For me, that would be a Practically Perfect Path to take, my own personal *Yellow Brick Road*.

I hope this book helps you on your leadership journey. Keep the Wicked Witch out of your head and always stay Playful in a good pair of shoes!

ACKNOWLEDGMENTS

Wow—what a journey! This book would not have been possible without the incredible people who have shaped my life and leadership.

To **Eric**, my best friend and biggest cheerleader—you have stood by me through every challenge, every crazy idea, and every new dream. Your belief in me never wavers, and I am endlessly grateful for you.

To my **DKZ Tribe**, the heartbeat of everything I do—your passion and commitment make magic happen every day. To **Melissa**, my biggest protector and hype girl, thank you for always having my back and lifting me up when I need it most. To **Jen G**, the yin to my yang, whose brilliance and balance keep me sane. To **Beth Cannon**, my little birdie, always there when I need a voice of reason or encouragement. To **Claire**, my little energizer bunny and productive ninja, and to my **Bozeman and Utah Tribe**—you are the soul of our community, and I cherish you all.

To **Julie Roy** my crazy but wickedly smart and kind side kick, mentor and role model. Thank you for paving the way and always putting family first. To **Beth Cannon** my little bird who always gives me advice, inspires me and shows me to love of Jesus!

Thank you **Jessie Kate Bui** from storymedium.com for helping me heal through storytelling and come up with creative ideas to start this book.

To **My Sweet Sarah**, whose heart and dedication remind me why we do this work. To **Kara**, for her hilarious, crazy, and perfectly timed humor—because leadership should always come with a little laughter.

To **Lil**, for her creative accountability and for pushing me to get this book done when I needed a nudge (or a shove). To **Alix Hall**, my sister from another mister, my travel buddy, and one of the greatest gifts life has given me—thank you for all you've taught me. To **Hillary Hartling**, whose branding genius helped me bring my vision to life and make this book truly me.

To **my grandma**, for teaching me how to be a wife, a mom, and now a grandma. You showed me how to love my family fiercely and fight for them even when they can't fight for themselves. To **God**, for being my guiding light through every season.

To **my mom**, for her resilience and playful nature—thank you for showing me how to find joy even in the hardest times. To **my brother Danny**, my rock growing up, my friend forever, and my favorite travel buddy. To **my sister Heidi**, for her creativity, artistic soul, and thoughtfulness—you inspire me. To my **sister-in-law Faby**, for her brilliant mind and for always reminding me to never quit—your wisdom and support mean the world to me.

To **my dad, Steve**, for choosing to raise us with love and Godly principles, shaping the foundation of who I am today. To **my grandpa**, my first leadership and business inspiration, and the kindest man who ever lived—I carry your lessons with me every day.

To **my bonus mama, Kristi,** whose never-ending business ideas, love for all things beautiful, and legendary hostess skills make every moment feel special.

To **John Maxwell,** whose leadership wisdom has shaped so much of my journey. To **Lori Buxton,** who first inspired me to share my ECE knowledge from a stage—your encouragement gave me the confidence to step into the spotlight. To **Kris Murray,** for giving me a chance as a coach and mentoring me in all things working on the business, not in it. Your guidance changed the trajectory of my leadership.

To **my Leadership Team,** my artery—without you, the vision wouldn't come to life. To **my teachers,** who take my dreams and turn them into reality for countless children, making the magic of play a priority every single day.

To **Krista,** my business mentor, for always challenging me to think bigger. To **my editor, Lil Barcaski and the team at GWN Publishing,** for helping bring this book to life. To **Ayrah,** my incredible virtual assistant who has been by my side for so long, navigating every season of growth with grace and patience.

To **Sherry Phillips and Tym Smith,** my crazy fun friends and brilliant business minds who inspire me with their passion and drive for professional development. To **Vernon Mason,** my sweet and hilarious friend and mentor—thank you for always making me laugh and for your smart insight on what the next best step is.

To **all my AELL EIS friends,** especially **Class B** (even though I wasn't cool enough to be Class B!). You have been my support system, my friends, and my *phone-a-friend* lifeline, especially through the dark days of COVID.

This book was not written alone—it was built on the love, support, and wisdom of so many. **From the bottom of my heart, thank you all for being part of my story.** This book is as much yours as it is mine.

fills her with pride, and she is absolutely loving her new title as Gigi to her grandson, Baby Zeke, her greatest hope for the future.

Rachel lives on a beautiful lake in Montana, where she finds inspiration in nature, family, and the quiet magic of the water. When she's not coaching, leading, or speaking, you can find her traveling, designing, mentoring, and bringing big, bold ideas to life—always with a little sparkle, a lot of passion, and an unstoppable drive to create impact.

Connect with Rachel:

WEBSITE: www.visiontreeleadership.com

FACEBOOK: facebook.com/RachelSupallaECE

INSTAGRAM: instagram.com/rachelsupalla_childcareexpert